Primary Partners®

Sharing Time

My Family Can Be Forever

12 Learning Activities and Bite-Size Memorize Scripture Posters
Preview of *Sharing Time Treasures*, 87 More Learning Activities to Match Theme
Preview of *Gospel Fun* Activities, 8 More Learning Activities to Match Theme

"My Family Can Be Forever" Sharing Time Themes 1-12

1. I Am a Child of God
2. The Family Is Central to Heavenly Father's Plan
3. Jesus Christ Makes it Possible for Me to Live with Heavenly Father Again
4. Families Can Be Happy When They Follow Jesus Christ
5. Family Members Have Important Responsibilities
6. Heavenly Father Teaches Me How to Strengthen Family
7. Temples Unite Families
8. Faith, Prayer, Repentance, and Forgiveness Can Strengthen My Family
9. Respect, Love, Work, and Wholesome Recreation Can Strengthen My Family
10. Prophets Teach Me How to Strengthen My Family
11. Keeping the Sabbath Day Holy Can Strengthen My Family
12. My Family Is Blessed When We Remember Jesus Christ

Introducing the Author and Illustrator, Creators of the Following Series of Books and CD-ROMS:

Primary Partners® (lesson match activities): *Nursery 1 & 2, CTR A, CTR B, Old Testament, New Testament, Book of Mormon, Doctrine & Covenants;*
Primary Partners® SHARING TIME: *Sharing Time, Sharing Time Treasures, Singing Fun, Primary Partners*® *"Faith in God" Activity Days;*
Young Women: Young Women Fun-tastic! Activities for Manual 1, Manual 2, Manual 3, and *Young Women Fun-tastic! Personal Progress Motivators;*
FAMILY HOME EVENING & PRIMARY:
Gospel Fun Activities, Gospel Games, Super Singing Activities, Super Little Singers, File-Folder Family Home Evenings, and *Home-spun Fun Family Home Evenings*

Mary Ross, Author

Mary Ross is an energetic mother and has been a Primary, Young Women, and Relief Society teacher and leader. She loves to help children and young women have a good time while learning. She has studied acting, modeling, and voice. Her varied interests include writing, creating activities and children's parties, and cooking. Mary and her husband Paul live with their daughter Jennifer in Sandy, Utah.

Jennette Guymon-King, Illustrator

Jennette Guymon-King studied graphic arts and illustration at Utah Valley College and the University of Utah. She served a mission in Japan. Jennette enjoys sports, reading, cooking, art, gardening, and freelance illustrating. Jennette and her husband Clayton live in Riverton, Utah. They are the proud parents of their daughter Kayla Mae, and sons Levi and Carson.

Copyright © 2003 by Mary H. Ross and Jennette Guymon-King
All Rights Reserved
Covenant Communications, Inc.
American Fork, Utah

Printed in the United States of America
First Printing: November 2003

Primary Partners® *Sharing Time "My Family Can Be Forever"*
ISBN 1-59156-364-X

—This product is neither sponsored nor endorsed by The Church of Jesus Christ of Latter-day Saints.
Acknowledgments: Thanks to Inspire Graphics (www.inspiregraphics.com) for Lettering Delights fonts.

INTRODUCTION
Primary Partners
SHARING TIME
Theme: My Family Can Be Forever

This sharing-time theme, "My Family Can Be Forever," is based on "The Family: A Proclamation to the World." President Gordon B. Hinckley said, "Why do we have this proclamation on the family now? Because the family is under attack. All across the world families are falling apart. The place to begin to improve society is in the home. Children do, for the most part, what they are taught. We are trying to make the world better by making the family stronger" (from *Teachings of Gordon B. Hinckley*, 209).

This volume of teaching ideas can be used year after year for Primary sharing time as well as for family home evening to teach children about strengthening the family.

The lessons will increase children's desires to be close to and support their families. They will want to be strong in the gospel so they can have an eternal families and enjoy the blessings of the temple. They will learn where they came from and why they are here living in a family. They will learn ways they can return with honor to live with Heavenly Father and Jesus again as eternal families.

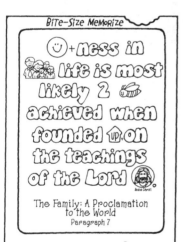

If you use the activities for family home evening, they will help reinforce what children are learning in Primary.

Teaching couldn't be easier with these 12 post-and-present activities and Bite-size Memorize posters (see left) that represent the 12 "My Family Can Be Forever . . ." themes. Simply copy, color, laminate, and cut out the visuals, then follow the instructions. You will also find small Bite-size Memorize scriptures to copy and give to children to match each theme.

All patterns and instructions from this book are available to print from CD-ROM (shown right) in color or black and white.

Other teaching books and CD-ROMs created for the 2004 theme "My Family Can Be Forever" are described below, and outlined on the following page and in the back of this book. Use them for sharing time, family home evening, or classroom presentations. Each of the following books are also available on CD-ROM so you can print the images in color or black and white.

- The *Gospel Fun Activities* book is in full color and ready to use. Simply tear out the perforated pages, cut out the visuals, and you have an instant presentation for sharing time or family home evening (p. 136-137).

- The *Primary Partners Sharing Time Treasures* contains 87 activities. These are all previewed in the back of this book. Simply copy and enlarge them to present to large groups, or use actual size for family home evening or individual handouts (p. 128-135).

- The *Primary Partners Singing Fun!* contains visuals for each song, plus activities to motivate children to sing. Also, singing leaders, see the back of this book to preview two more singing activity books: *Super Singing Activities* and *Super Little Singers* (full color and ready to use—see p. 138).

More 2004 Sharing-Time Theme Books and CD-ROMS:
Theme: "My Family Can Be Forever"

	Primary Partners Sharing Time Treasures book & CD	*Gospel Fun Activities* all-color book and CD-ROM (see back pages)	*Primary Partners Singing Fun!* book and CD-ROM
*See previews for *Primary Partners Sharing Time Treasures* and *Gospel Fun Activities* books and CD-ROMS below and in the back of this book. **2004 Themes**			
1. I Am a Child of God	1. Eight activities to help children know they are a child of God		1. "I Am a Child of God" & "I Know My Father Lives"
2. The Family Is Central to Heavenly Father's Plan	2. Six activities to learn of Heavenly Father's Plan		2. "Love Is Spoken Here"
3. Jesus Makes It Possible to Live with Heavenly Father Again	3. Eight activities to help children live the teachings of Jesus		3. "He Sent His Son"
4. Families Can Be Happy When They Follow Jesus Christ	4. Six activities to help children learn to be happy with their families	4. Activity 9: Happy Henry and Miserable Mack Body-Building Puzzles	4. "I Feel My Savior's Love"
5. Family Members Have Important Responsibilities	5. Six activities to learn responsibilities in the home		5. "The Family" and "A Happy Family"
6. Heavenly Father Teaches Me How to Strengthen My Family	6. Eight activities to learn the teachings of Heavenly Father that strengthen the family	6. Use Activities—1: Annabell's Accountable Cow Farm, 2: CTR Tools Match Game, 3: Commandment Maze, 10: Second-Coming Suitcase	6. "Home Can Be a Heaven on Earth"
7. Temples Unite Families	7. Seven activities to tell how temples unite families	7. Use Activities—4: Strong-and-Wilting-Plant Match Game, 5: Find-the-Light Situation Spotlight	7. "Families Can Be Together Forever"
8. Faith, Prayer, Repentance, And Forgiveness Can Strengthen My Family	8. Eight activities to learn faith, prayer, repentance, etc. to make a strong family	8. Use Activities 1, 2, and 3 (see #6 above)	8. "I Pray in Faith"
9. Respect, Love, Work, and Wholesome Recreation Can Strengthen My Family	9. Eight activities to learn respect, compassion, love, and more	9. Use Activity 6: Trail-to-Holy-Ghost-Town Game.	Plus activities to motivating singing
10. Prophets Teach Me How to Strengthen My Family	10. Eight activities to learn what the prophets teach about families	10. Use Activities 4 and 5 (see #7 above), 11: My-Service-Garden Game to Plant Acts of Service	
11. Keeping the Sabbath Day Holy Can Strengthen My Family	11. Six activities to learn how a family is blessed as they remember Jesus		
12. My Family Is Blessed When We Remember Jesus Christ	12. Six activities to help children know and remember Jesus	12. Use Activities—7: Missionary Kite Maze 8: Missionary Fish Find 12: Testimony Foundation	

Table of Contents
Primary Partners® Sharing Time
"My Family Can Be Forever"

Theme 1   I Am a Child of God

SCRIPTURE TO MEMORIZE: Memorize *The Family: A Proclamation to the World* Bite-size Memorize poster on p. 2 (shown right). Give children a copy of the small Bite-size Memorize on page 3 or print from CD-ROM.*

SONG: Sing "I Am a Child of God" in the *Children's Songbook*, p. 5. This song is illustrated in *Primary Partners® Singing Fun!—My Family Can Be Forever* book and CD-ROM.

LESSON: Ask, "How do we know we are children of God and that He loves us?" Answer this question using the scriptures, Primary lessons, and sources below to teach.

- I am a child of God. He loves me, and I love Him (Romans 8:16; 1 John 4:19; *Primary 2—CTR A*, lesson 3).
- I can pray to Heavenly Father anytime, anywhere. I am trying to remember and follow Jesus (3 Nephi 14:7-8; Alma 34:19-27).
- I lived in heaven with Heavenly Father and Jesus before I was born. Heavenly Father and Jesus want us to live as families in heaven (Moses 6:51; Moses 1:39; *Primary 3—CTR B*, lesson 35).
- I am created in the image of God. My body is a temple (Genesis 1:27; 1 Corinthians 3:16-17; "My Gospel Standards," paragraphs 5, 8-11).

MORE IDEAS: See More Sharing-Time Activities (Theme 1) previewed in the back of this book, available in the *Primary Partners® Sharing Time Treasures—My Family Can Be Forever* book or CD-ROM (to print images in color or black and white).

Activity: Heavenly Father Loves Me (Heavenly Mailbox—Letters from and to Heavenly Father)

OBJECTIVE: Tell children, "Heavenly Father loves each of you. As you read the scriptures you will learn that He loves you and wants you to return to Him. Let's look into the *Heaven-Sent Mailbox* to see if we can find some love letters from Heavenly Father. Then, as you think of what to write, you can write a love letter to Him. How will He get the letter? He knows every thought you have and every wish of your heart.

TO MAKE VISUALS: *Copy, color, cut out the visuals (p. 4-14), putting together the mailbox by folding and gluing tabs where indicated. Fold mailbox latch so the top flips up and the bottom flap flips down. Use a paperclip or Velcro to hold flap closed. Place each letter in a small envelope and seal it so children can open each letter to read.

TO PRESENT:

1. Place the *Heaven-Sent Mailbox* in front with letters from Heavenly Father inside. Have children take turns pulling out a letter, opening it, and reading it aloud. Talk about each.

2. Tell children ways they can express appreciation and love to Heavenly Father. Give each of them a heart-shaped stationery on which they can write a love letter to Heavenly Father. Then place it back in the mailbox or post on the wall. *Option:* Children can draw a picture of something they are grateful for. Read these letters, without reading the child's name, so others can know what is written.

All images can be printed in full color and black and white using the CD-ROM:
Primary Partners Sharing Time—My Family Can Be Forever.

👁 M a 👦👧 of God. 👁 know heavenly Father 💗Loves me, and 👁 💗Love Him. 👁 🥤 🙅 2 heavenly Father NE+🕐, NE+where. 👁 M trying 2 remember and follow.

Jesus Christ

Faith in God guidebook

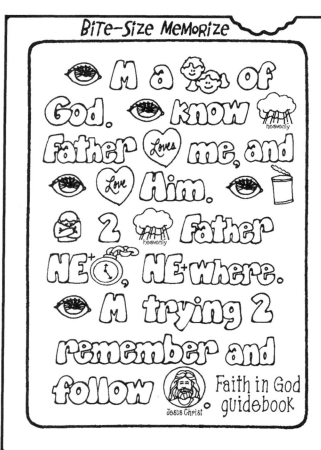

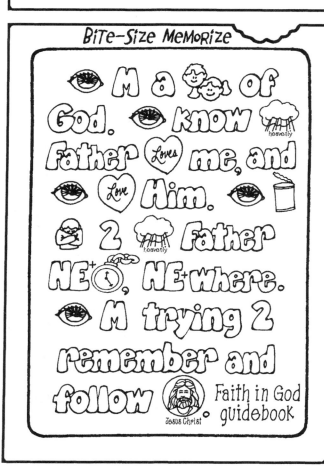

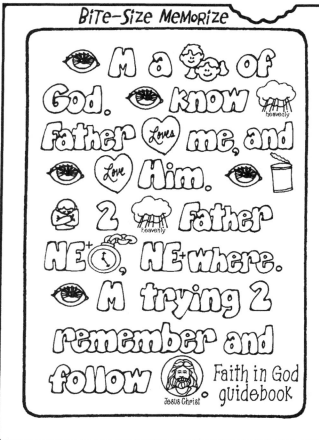

Side piece A.

Fold back and glue to base.

Side piece B

Glue to Part A.

Heaven-Sent Mailbox

Fold back and glue to base.

Back piece

I Love My
Heavenly Father!

Fold back and glue to base.

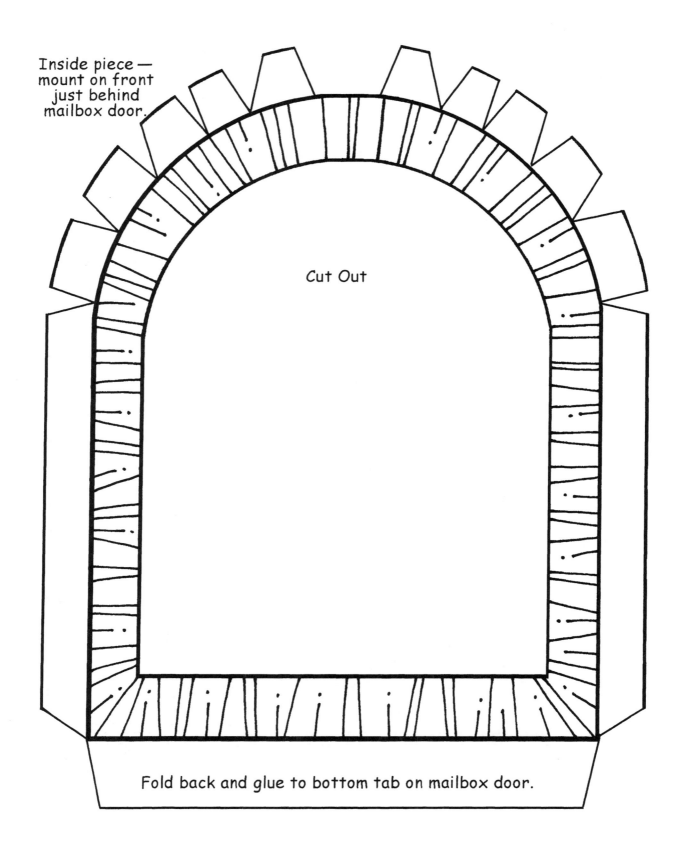

Inside piece—
mount on front
just behind
mailbox door.

Cut Out

Fold back and glue to bottom tab on mailbox door.

Attach to center front of side pieces A and B, and fold where indicated.

Fold back.

Glue here

Mailbox Door

Fold forward at both places.

My Heavenly Father Loves Me!

Fold back and glue to base

Base

Glue front piece and front-door tabs here.

Glue side tab here.

Glue side tab here.

Glue back-piece tab here.

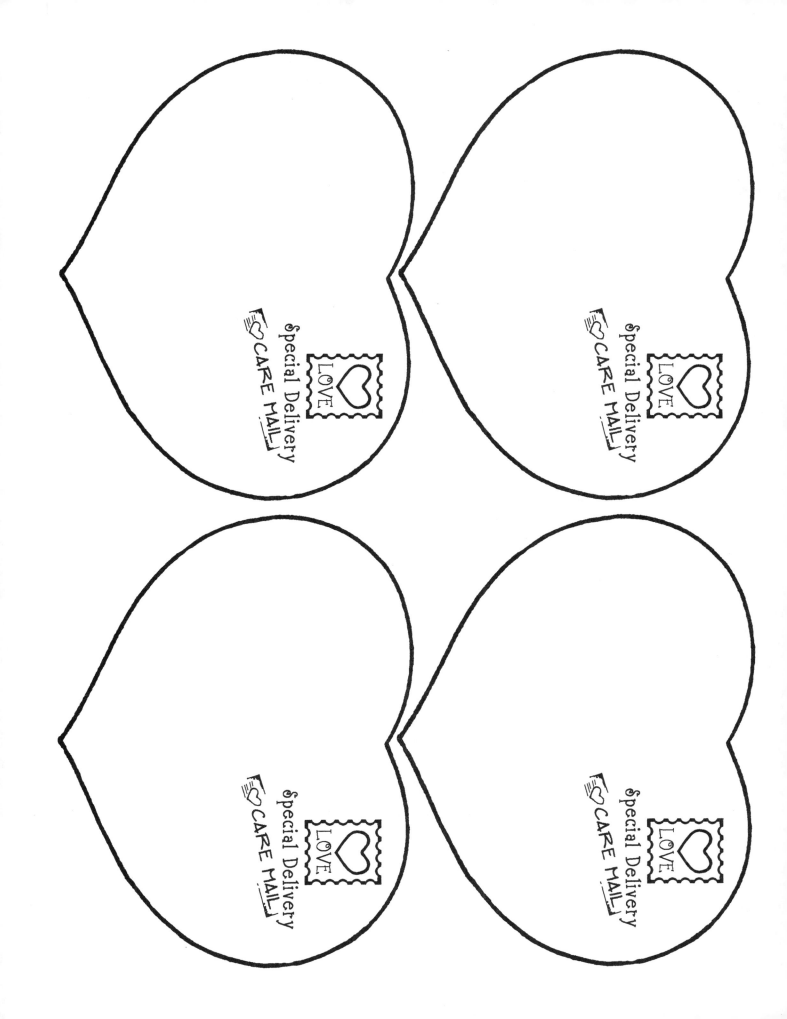

My Dear Children:

Jesus is the first spirit born to me, and He is your elder brother. Jesus chose to follow my plan and volunteered to be your Savior.

To gain experience for Himself, Jesus was born on the earth to earthly parents. He gave the perfect example for all to follow. He lived all of my commandments, and was kind and forgiving. He loved and served others and taught about my plan. He then suffered and died so that everyone would be able to live again.

If you always remember Jesus and live as He lived, you can return to live with me someday. Because of Jesus, you can repent when you have done wrong. Please follow Jesus so you can return to me.

— Love, Heavenly Father

My Dear Children:

It is true that your spirit lived in heaven with me a long time ago. You lived there with people you loved. One day you learned about my wonderful plan and shouted for joy! You wanted to come to earth, so I sent you to live with your family.

When you arrived on earth, your spirit entered your body, making your body come to life. Your body of flesh and bones is like mine, created in my image. It is a temple where your spirit lives, so I want you to take care of yourself so you will live long upon the earth and be happy.

When you die, your body will go to the spirit world. Then, on the day of resurrection, your spirit will reenter your body and they will never be separated again. Take care of yourself and remember that I love you.

— Love, Heavenly Father

My Dear Children:

When you read the scriptures you will read of my words and of those who are inspired to teach you of my plan.

In the scriptures you will learn of my commandments. You will learn of those who kept my commandments and those who chose not to. You will learn of actions that made people happy and actions that made them sad.

If you read the scriptures each day, you will feel the great love I have for you and you will be guided back to me. I love you.

– Love, Heavenly Father

My Dear Children:

When you chose to come to earth, you knew you would not remember your heavenly home. By forgetting your life with me, it is necessary for you to walk by faith. But if you believe in me, I can guide you.

I want you to pray to me anytime and anywhere. I will always be there to hear your every prayer. Pray when you are sad or frightened, pray when you feel confused or angry, and pray when you are grateful and happy.

You can pray aloud or silently because I can understand your thoughts. If you look to me, I will answer your prayers and guide you throughout your life. I love you and want you to be happy and return to me.

– Love, Heavenly Father

My Dear Children:

Each one of you are special. I blessed all of you with different talents and abilities.

When you lived with me you worked to develop many talents. Now that you are on the earth, you should continue to learn and grow.

I want you to pray to learn what special talents are yours and what great things can happen when you use your special gifts.

When you are older, you can also receive a patriarchal blessing which will tell you about the many talents you have.

Listen carefully and learn all that you can. Then, when you discover your talents, I will bless you as you develop them and use them. I gave you talents so that you can serve others and enjoy your life on the earth.

— Love, Heavenly Father

My Dear Children:

You are part of my forever family. Families can be together forever when parents are married in the temple and children are either born under the covenant or sealed to parents in the temple.

I want all of my children on the earth to enjoy the blessings of the temple. This way they can be with their families forever, as husband and wife and children. If you continue to obey my commandments, death cannot separate your family. Then, when you return to heaven, we will all be one big happy family.

I want you to be thoughtful and kind to your earthly family. They love you and want you to be with them forever.

— Love, Heavenly Father

My Dear Children:

Long before you came to earth there was a great gathering in heaven. You were all there when I presented my plan.

Satan wanted to force you to choose good, and desired that he have the glory. However, Jesus had great love for each of you and wanted to preserve your agency so you can choose for yourselves. Jesus knew that my plan was the only way we could truly progress and be happy.

The spirits who rebelled and followed Satan did not receive a body. The spirits who chose to follow Jesus are able to come to earth and receive a body. You are one of those who chose to follow Jesus.

If you learn about Jesus and follow His example, you will find it easy to make good choices and be happy. You may be tempted to make a wrong choice, but you have the power to say "no" and choose the right. This way you can return to live with me again someday. I love you dearly.

— Love, Heavenly Father

My Dear Children:

When you came to earth, I did not want you to be alone, so I sent a member of the Godhead to guide and comfort you. This special spirit is the Holy Ghost.

After you are baptized you are given this special gift. The Holy Ghost dwells in your heart. He will prompt you to do good and will testify to you of truth. He will give you peace in times of trial.

Listen to His still small voice and follow your feelings as He helps you to make the right choices.

If you obey my commandments you can always have the Holy Ghost as your companion and you will have a peaceful feeling that will bring you happiness. Stay true.

— Love, Heavenly Father

Theme 2   The Family Is Central to Heavenly Father's Plan

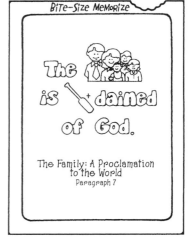

BITE-SIZE MEMORIZE

The [family] is [or]dained of God.

The Family: A Proclamation to the World
Paragraph 7

SCRIPTURE TO MEMORIZE: Memorize *The Family: A Proclamation to the World* Bite-size Memorize poster on p. 16 (shown right). Give children a copy of the small Bite-size Memorize on page 17 or print from CD-ROM.*

SONG: Sing "Love Is Spoken Here" in the *Children's Songbook*, p. 190. This song is illustrated in *Primary Partners® Singing Fun!—My Family Can Be Forever* book and CD-ROM.

LESSON: Ask, "How is the family part of Heavenly Father's plan?" Answer question using the scriptures, Primary lessons, and sources below to teach.

• I have a family here on earth (*Primary 2—CTR A*, lesson 6).

• "Marriage between man and woman is essential to His eternal plan" (*The Family: A Proclamation to the World*, D&C 49:15).

• "Parents have a sacred duty to rear their children in love and righteousness" (*The Family: A Proclamation to the World*, see also Proverbs 22:6; *Primary 3*, lessons 28, 39).

• The priesthood blesses, serves, and strengthens my family (D&C 121:36, 41-43; Abraham 2:10-11; *Primary 3—CTR B*, lesson 9).

MORE IDEAS: See More Sharing-Time Activities (Theme 2) previewed in the back of this book, available in the *Primary Partners® Sharing Time Treasures—My Family Can Be Forever* book or CD-ROM (to print images in color or black and white).

Activity: I'm Blessed with a Family (Bloomin'-Blessings Guessing Game)

OBJECTIVE: Tell children, "We are blessed to have a family. Let's play a guessing game to learn what our family does to bless us, and how we can bless our family to watch our family blossom and grow."

TO MAKE VISUALS: *Copy, color, cut out visuals (p. 18-23). Mount house scene and two fences on a poster, board, or wall, with flowers taped to different parts of the room, under chairs, or mixed up on the opposite side of the board or place in a container.

HOW MY FAMILY BLESSES ME

HOW I CAN BLESS MY FAMILY

TO PRESENT:

1. Have children take turns finding a flower and reading the blessing aloud.

2. Child tapes the flower in front one of the two fences: "How My Family Blesses Me," or "How I Can Bless My Family."

3. Encourage children to think of how their family is blessed this week and how they can help.

*All images can be printed in full color and black and white using the CD-ROM: *Primary Partners Sharing Time—My Family Can Be Forever.*

The [family picture] is [screwdriver] + dained of God.

The Family: A Proclamation
to the World
Paragraph 7

The is + dained of God.

The Family: A Proclamation to the World
Paragraph 7

Bite-Size Memorize

The is + dained of God.

The Family: A Proclamation to the World
Paragraph 7

Bite-Size Memorize

The is + dained of God.

The Family: A Proclamation to the World
Paragraph 7

Bite-Size Memorize

The is + dained of God.

The Family: A Proclamation to the World
Paragraph 7

Cut carefully along the inside of the dotted line.

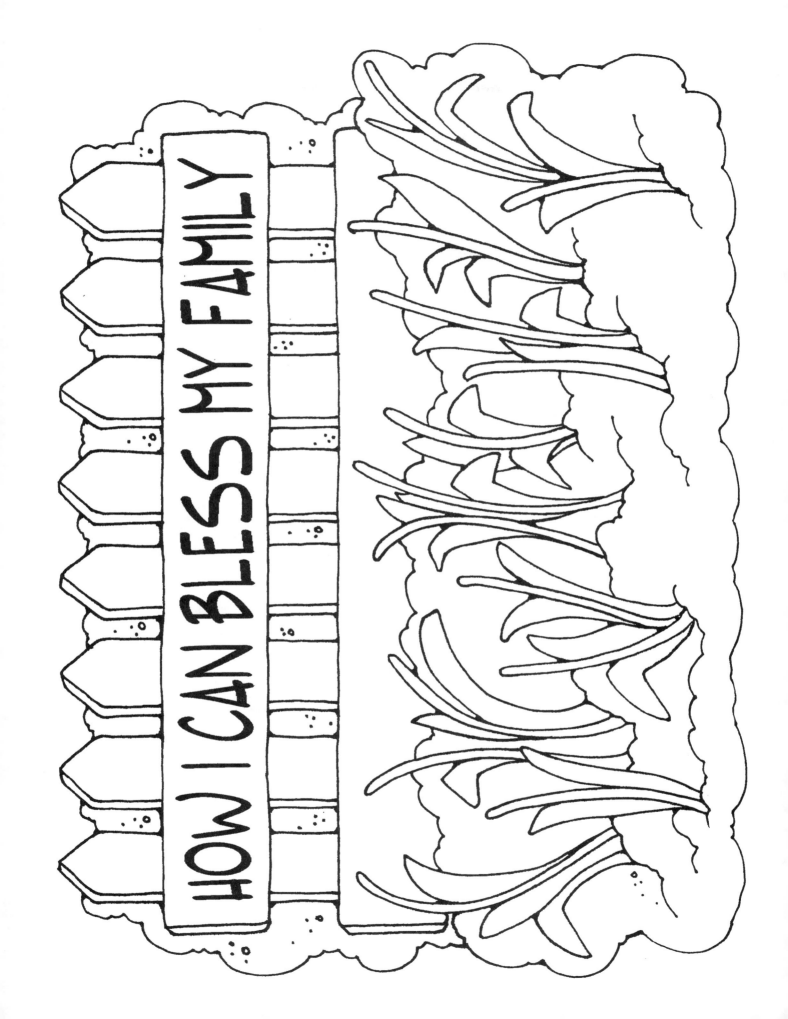

Be kind to my brother, so he will know I love him.

Water and weed the garden so we can have fresh vegetables to eat.

My parents teach me how to be kind by being kind to me.

When I was a baby, my father gave me a name and a blessing.

Be happy and helpful at family home evening each week.

Help do the dinner dishes so Mom can rest after a long day.

My mother takes care of me, and my father blesses me when I am really sick.

My father gives me a special father's blessing to help me do well in school.

Be honest so my family will trust me.

Seek good friends who are examples to me and my brothers and sisters.

My sister helps me find good friends so I can make right choices.

My family reads the scriptures together daily so I can gain a testimony.

Do not be critical; look for the good in each family member.

Be willing to forgive when a family member has hurt you.

My father teaches me how to fix my bike, so next time I can fix it myself.

My mother lets me babysit so I can learn to be a good parent someday.

Do my homework early so I don't keep my family up late.

Say thanks when a family member helps me so they will know that I'm grateful.

My father teaches me to work by having me help him clean the garage.

My mother teaches me how to fix a healthy meal so I can care for myself someday.

Be kind and thoughtful in what I do and say.

Be reverent during scripture study so my family can listen and learn.

When we have family prayer, I feel the love my family has for me.

When my parents are sealed in the temple, my family can be together forever.

Go to bed on time so I am not grumpy the next day.

Spend time with my family so they know that I care.

When my father spends time with me, it tells me that he loves me.

When my parents take me to church, I learn about Heavenly Father's special plan for me.

Theme 3   Jesus Christ Makes it Possible for Me to Live with Heavenly Father Again

SCRIPTURE TO MEMORIZE: Memorize the John 14:6 Bite-size Memorize poster on p. 25 (shown right). Give children a copy of the small Bite-size Memorize on page 26 or print from CD-ROM.*

SONG: Sing "He Sent His Son" in the *Children's Songbook*, p. 34. This song is illustrated in *Primary Partners® Singing Fun!—My Family Can Be Forever* book and CD-ROM.

LESSON: Ask, "How has Jesus made it possible for us to live with Heavenly Father again?" Answer this question using the scriptures, Primary lessons, and sources below to teach.

- Before I came to earth, I chose to follow Heavenly Father's plan *(Gospel Principles* chapters 2, 3; *Primary 2—CTR A*, lesson 4).
- Jesus Christ is our Savior. He atoned for my sins (Articles of Faith 1:3; *Primary 3—CTR B*, lesson 22).
- Because Jesus was resurrected, I will be resurrected (John 11:23; 1 Corinthians 15:22; *Primary 3—CTR B*, lesson 46).
- Choosing the right and following Jesus will help me return to Heavenly Father (3 Nephi 27:21-22; *Primary 3—CTR B*, lesson 27; "The Message: Return with Honor," *New Era*, Jan-Feb. 1979, 4, Elder Robert D. Hales).

MORE IDEAS: See More Sharing-Time Activities (Theme 3) previewed in the back of this book, available in the *Primary Partners® Sharing Time Treasures—My Family Can Be Forever* book or CD-ROM.*

Activity: I Can Return to Heavenly Father (Return-with-Honor Game)

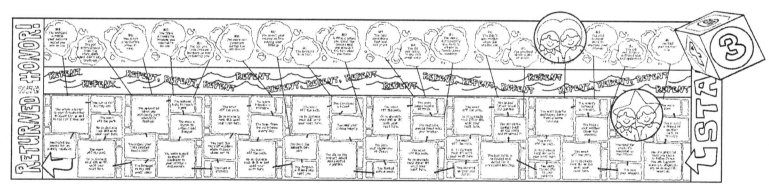

OBJECTIVE: Tell children, "Before we came to earth we lived with Heavenly Father and Jesus. We can return with honor by choosing the right and following Jesus each day."

TO MAKE VISUALS: *Copy, color, cut out, assemble, and laminate the visuals (p. 27-32). Post the game parts 1-6 on the board or posters as shown above. To make die, fold and glue tabs inside.

TO PRESENT:
- Divide into two teams, e.g., boys against girls, giving each team a marker to place at the START position.
- Teams take turns rolling the die and moving their marker the number of spaces on the path. They move along the path or off the path as follows (following the arrows):
- If they land on a right action they stay on the path, working their way to the RETURNED WITH HONOR sign.
- *Off the Path:* If they land on a wrong action they move off the path (designated by the number) onto the obstacle road. Then they read the rock and tell how they can repent of that action. When it's their turn again, they can roll the die and move, following the line from the rock back to the path.
- The first team to reach RETURNED WITH HONOR wins!

*All images can be printed in full color and black and white using the CD-ROM: *Primary Partners Sharing Time—My Family Can Be Forever.*

Saith N2 him, 👁 M the way, the truth, and the life: no 🧒 cometh N2 the Father, but by me.

John 14:6

Saith N2 him,  M the way the truth, and the life: no cometh N2 the Father, but by me.

John 14:6

Saith N2 him, M the way the truth, and the life: no cometh N2 the Father, but by me.

John 14:6

Saith N2 him, M the way the truth, and the life: no cometh N2 the Father, but by me.

John 14:6

Saith N2 him, M the way the truth, and the life: no cometh N2 the Father, but by me.

John 14:6

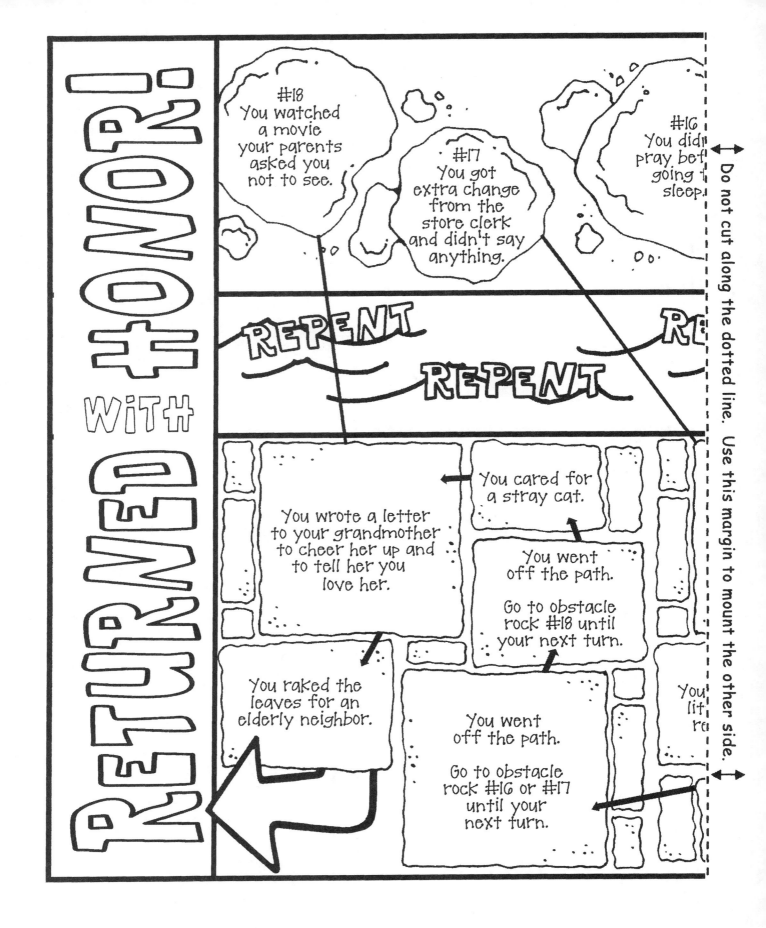

Do not cut along the dotted line. Use this margin to mount the other side.

Cut carefully along the inside of the dotted line.

#15
You tried a cigarette because you wanted to be cool.

#14
You hit your little brother because he was bothering you.

#13
You were not reverent during the sacrament.

REPENT, REPENT, REPENT, REPENT

You apologized when you accidentally hurt someone's feelings.

You worked hard to reach a goal.

You sang a hymn to erase a bad thought.

You went off the path.

Go to obstacle rock #15 until your next turn.

helped your tle brother ead a book.

You were a good example of kindness to your brothers and sisters.

You kept the Word of Wisdom when friends chose not to.

You listened to the still small voice.

You kept a promise.

You w off the

Go to ob rock #13 until y next t

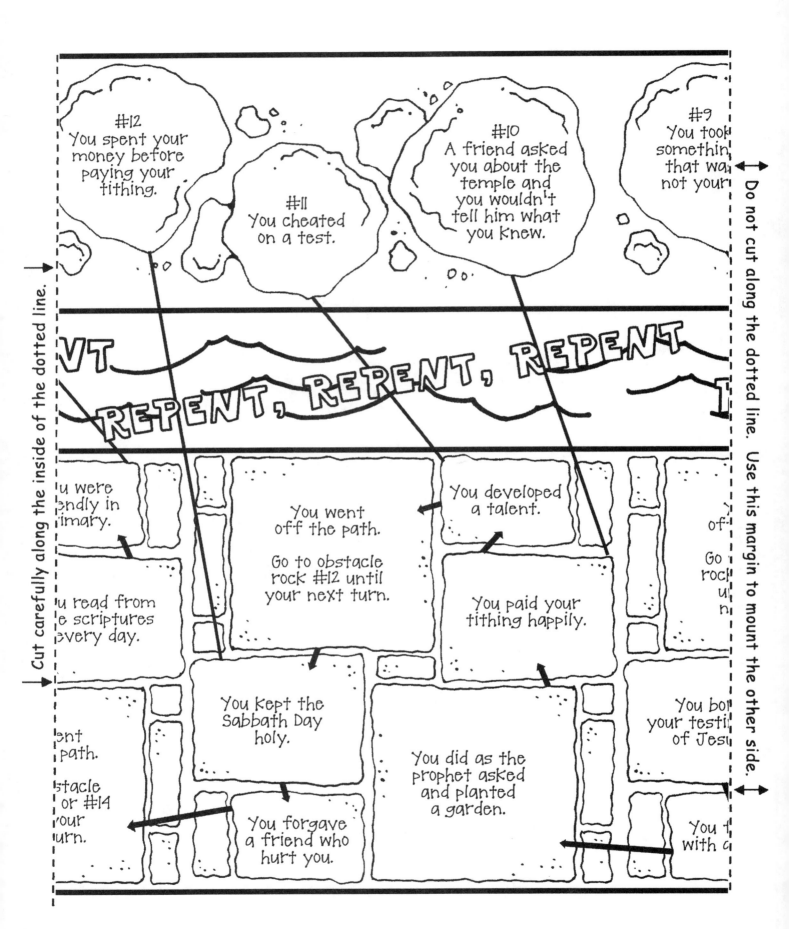

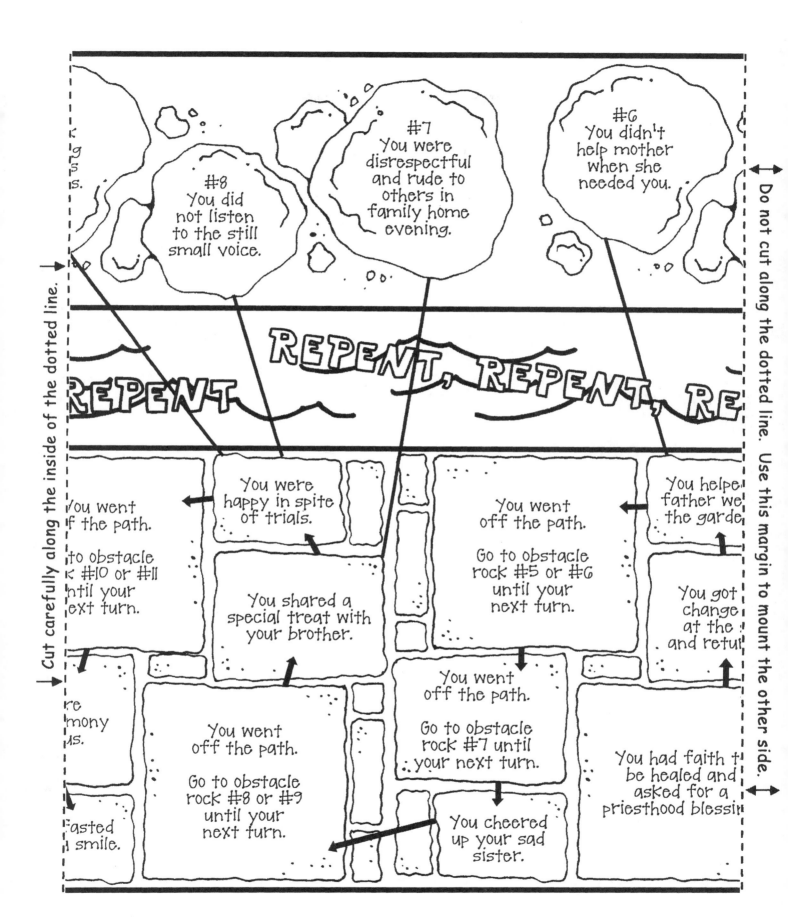

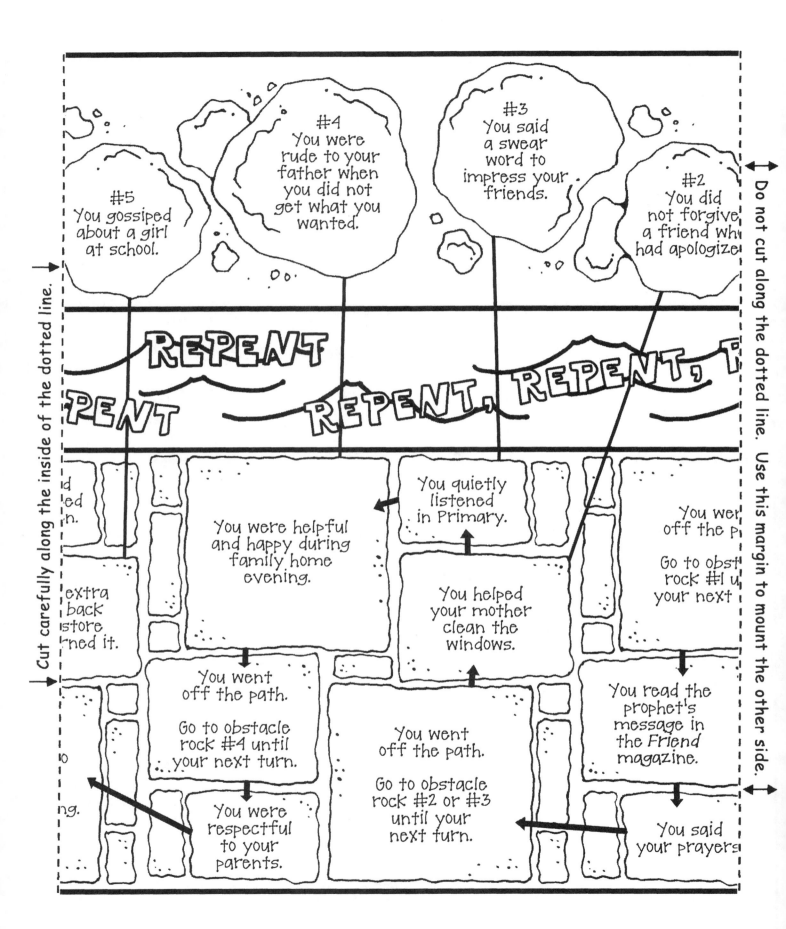

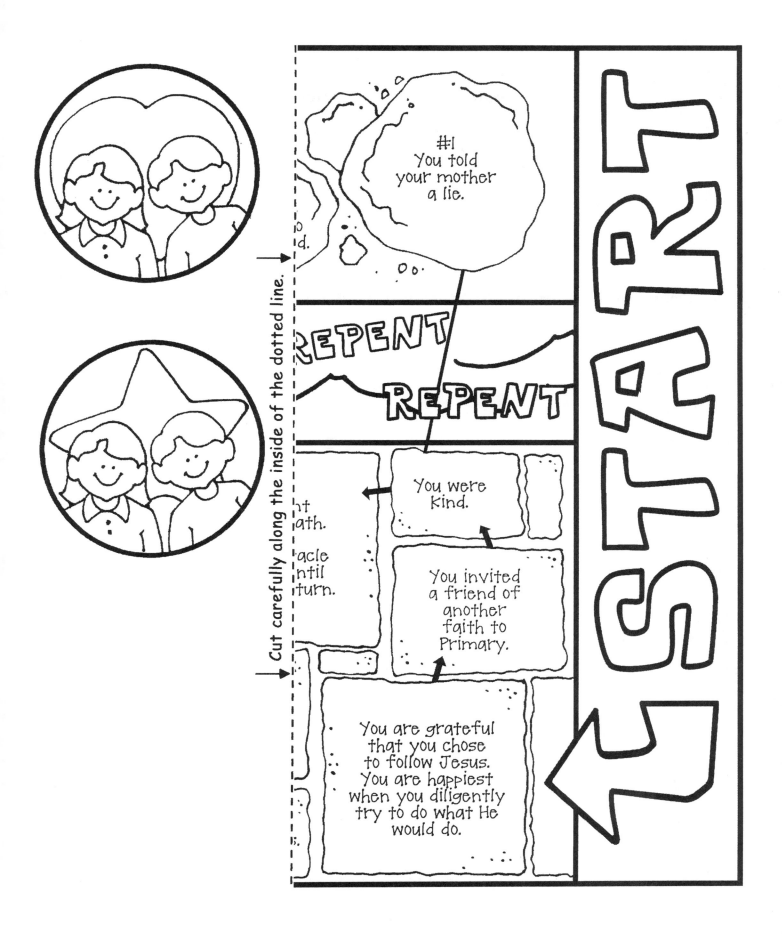

Theme 4   Families Can Be Happy When They Follow Jesus Christ

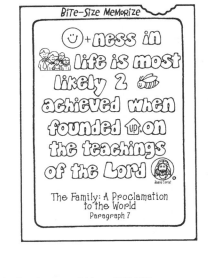

Bite-Size Memorize

☺+ness in 👨‍👩‍👧 life is most likely 2 🐝 achieved when founded up on the teachings of the Lord ✝.

The Family: A Proclamation to the World
Paragraph 7

SCRIPTURE TO MEMORIZE: Memorize *The Family: A Proclamation to the World* Bite-size Memorize poster on p. 36 (shown right). Give children a copy of the small Bite-size Memorize on page 37 or print from CD-ROM.*

SONG: Sing "I Feel My Savior's Love" in the *Children's Songbook*, p. 74. This song is illustrated in *Primary Partners® Singing Fun!—My Family Can Be Forever* book and CD-ROM.

LESSON: Ask, "How can families be happy when they follow Jesus?" Answer this question using the scriptures, Primary lessons, and sources below to teach.

- The Holy Ghost blesses my family and helps me follow Jesus Christ (Moroni 10:5; *Primary 3—CTR B*, lessons 12, 20).
- Obeying Heavenly Father's commandments and following Jesus helps my family be happy (Alma 37:35; *Primary 2—CTR A*, lessons 15, 30).
- Living "My Gospel Standards" helps me follow Jesus Christ (D&C 59:23; John 14:21).
- I can follow Jesus by being a peacemaker (Matthew 5:9; *Primary 2—CTR A*, lesson 22; *Primary 4—Book of Mormon*, lesson 34).

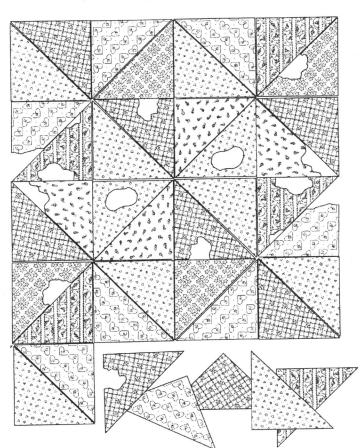

MORE IDEAS: See More Sharing-Time Activities (Theme 4) previewed in the back of this book, available in the *Primary Partners® Sharing Time Treasures—My Family Can Be Forever* book or CD-ROM (to print images in color or black and white).

Activity: My Family Can Be Happy (Comforts of Home— Family Quilting Bee)

OBJECTIVE: Tell children, "You and your family can be happy as you listen to the Holy Ghost and following the teachings of Jesus."

TO MAKE VISUALS: *Copy, color, and cut out four copies of the smooth-edged quilt pieces, two or three copies of the ragged-edged quilt pieces (as indicated), and one set of good-choice and bad-choice wordstrips (p. 38-46). Glue the good-choice wordstrips on the backs of the smooth-edge quilt pieces and the wrong-choice wordstrips on the backs of the ragged-edged quilt pieces. Mix up the quilt pieces and place in a container to draw from.

*All images can be printed in full color and black and white using the CD-ROM: *Primary Partners Sharing Time—My Family Can Be Forever.*

34

To Present Quilting Bee: CHOOSE FROM OPTION 1 OR 2 BELOW TO PRESENT

1. Tell children you are going to make a *Comforts of Home—Family Quilt* to learn ways we can make our family happy.
— The smooth-edged quilt pieces show actions that make your family happy because you are listening to the Holy Ghost and following Jesus.
— The ragged-edged quilt pieces show actions that make your family sad because you are not listening to the Holy Ghost or following Jesus.

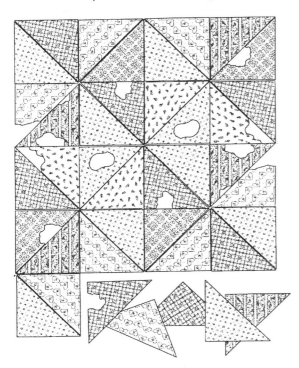

2. Divide into two teams. Have teams take turns drawing a quilt block and reading the action on the back. Then have them tape the quilt block on the board to make a quilt, using one of the following presentation choices.
3. Award a point for each good-choice (smooth-edged) block chosen. When all are gathered, add up the points and announce the winning team.

Presentation Option #1 (shown left):

1. Place all pieces in the quilt randomly, not trying to fit them on the quilt, creating a crazy mixed up quilt because the ragged-edged quilt pieces (bad-choices) won't fit evenly to make a comfortable quilt.
2. When actions are read and quilt pieces placed, look at the quilt and talk about how the bad choices (ragged-edged quilt pieces) make an uncomfortable family quilt. It is not soft, smooth, and cozy because there are holes everywhere.
3. Suggest they take away these ragged-edged pieces (bad choices) to make their family quilt comfortable, leaving only the

smooth-edged (good choices) quilt pieces. Have children help you arrange it this way, asking them to leave only the best pieces.
4. Now admire the finished product, asking them to think of ways they can make their home comfortable and peaceful like this family quilt.

Presentation Option #2 (shown right):

Build the quilt, placing only the good-choice (smooth-edged) quilt pieces on the quilt and the bad pieces to the side, following steps 3 and 4 above.

Take-Home Option:

Give each child a piece of quilted fabric to remind them to look for ways they can make their family feel comfortable and happy. Remind them they can do this by listening to the Holy Ghost and following the teachings of Jesus.

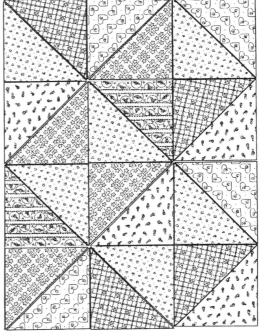

*All images can be printed in full color and black and white using the CD-ROM:
Primary Partners Sharing Time—My Family Can Be Forever.

☺+ness in life is most likely 2 🐝 achieved when founded UP+on the teachings of the Lord.

Jesus Christ

The Family: A Proclamation to the World
Paragraph 7

☺+ness in life is most likely 2 🐝 achieved when founded UP+on the teachings of the Lord. Jesus Christ

The Family: A Proclamation to the World
Paragraph 7

Bite-Size Memorize

☺+ness in life is most likely 2 🐝 achieved when founded UP+on the teachings of the Lord. Jesus Christ

The Family: A Proclamation to the World
Paragraph 7

Bite-Size Memorize

☺+ness in life is most likely 2 🐝 achieved when founded UP+on the teachings of the Lord. Jesus Christ

The Family: A Proclamation to the World
Paragraph 7

Bite-Size Memorize

☺+ness in life is most likely 2 🐝 achieved when founded UP+on the teachings of the Lord. Jesus Christ

The Family: A Proclamation to the World
Paragraph 7

Make 4 copies.

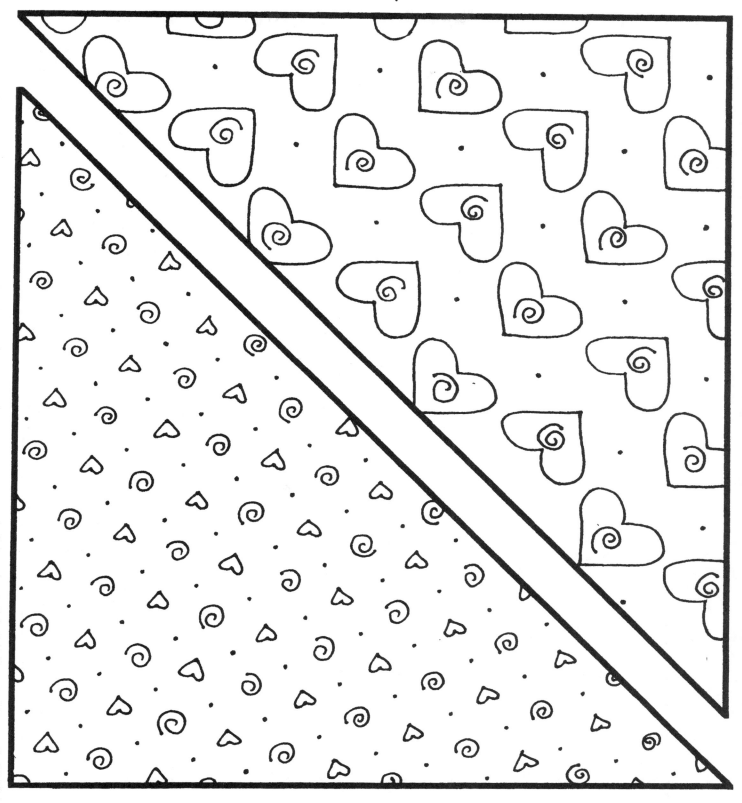

Make 4 copies.

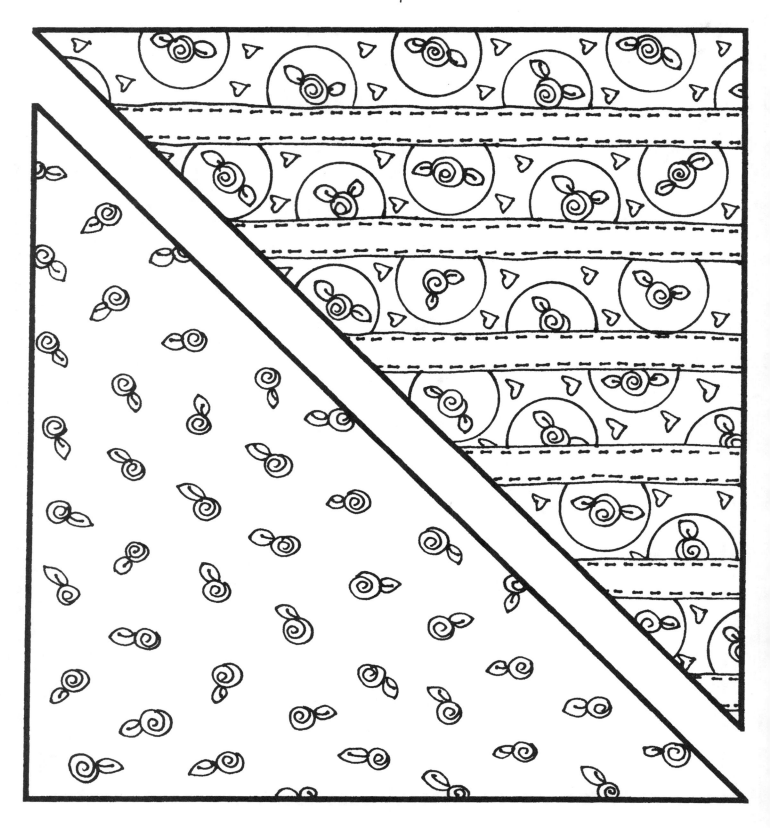

Make 4 copies.

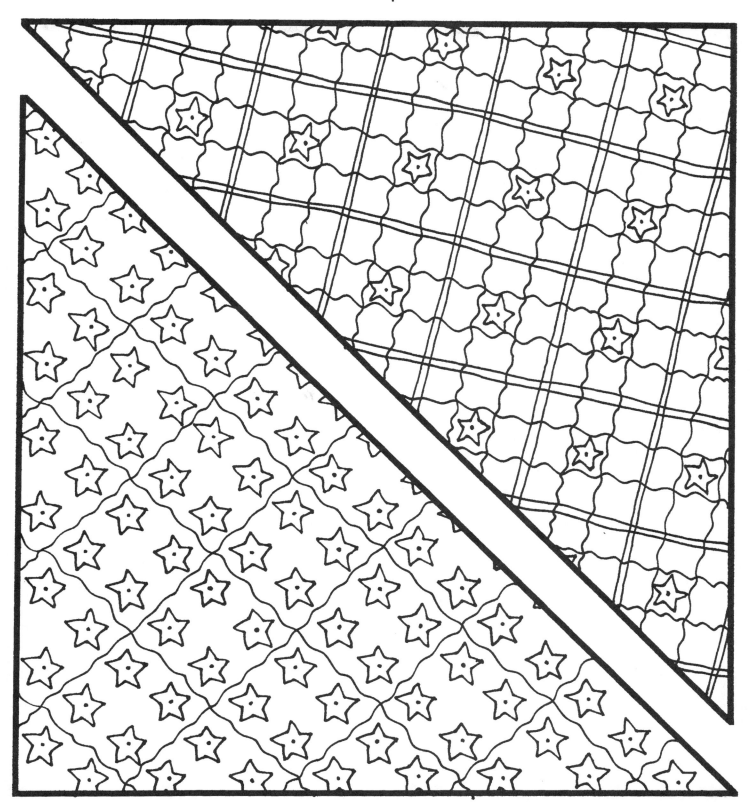

Make 3 copies..

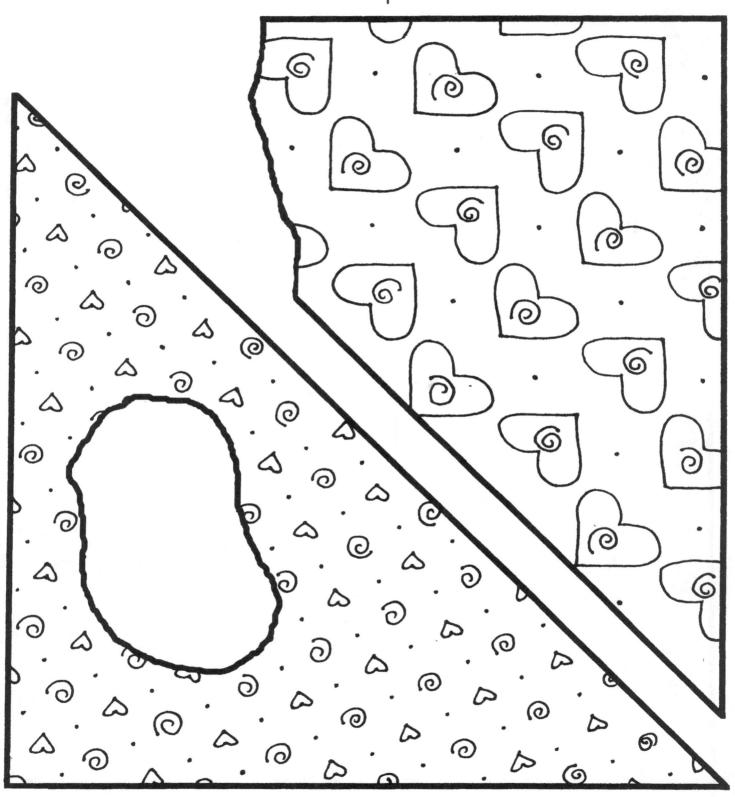

Make 3 copies.

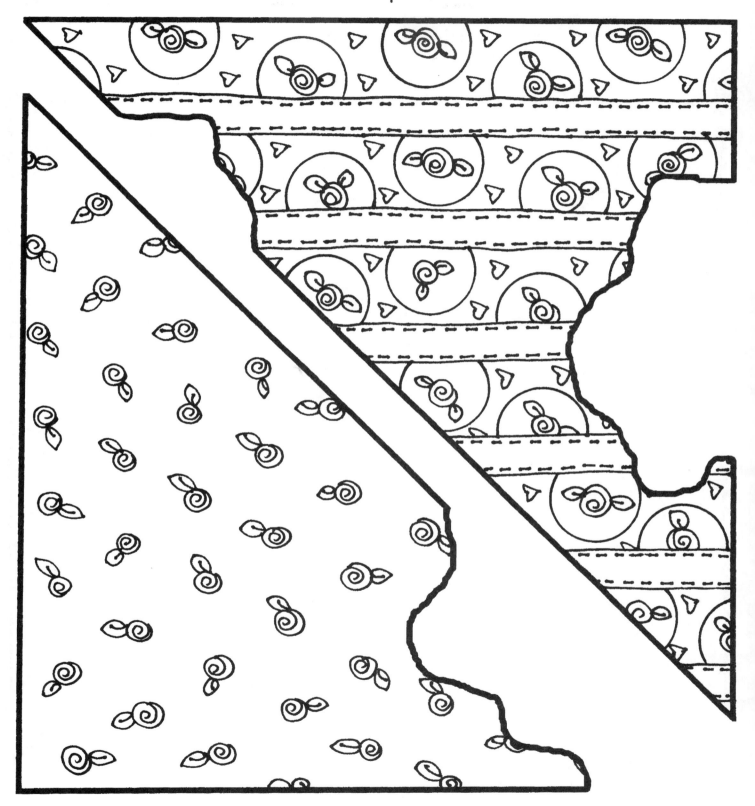

Make <u>only</u> 2 copies.

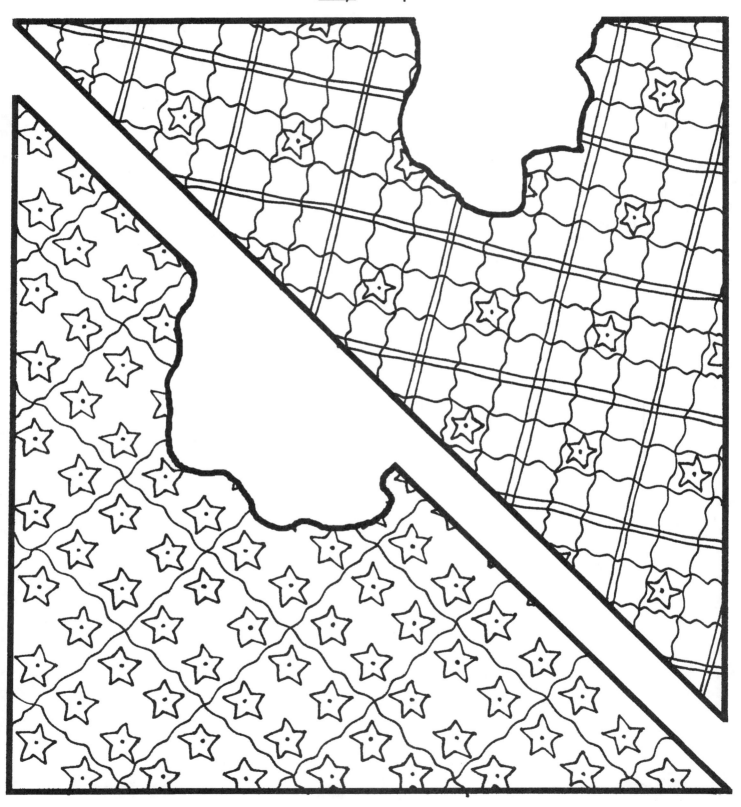

Sandra could see her brother wanted a special toy, so she gave up buying a toy for herself so there would be enough money.

Levi's brother wanted to draw pictures on the table cloth, so Levi got some paper for him to use instead.

Nicole's family moved to a new town and her brother was worried he wouldn't make friends. She told him to be the first to say "hi" and tell them who he was. It helped him make friends.

Jeff tried to learn more about his family by asking them questions about what they liked and didn't like. It helped them to feel closer.

Hilda learned how to make book covers out of fabric, so she made one for each family member's scriptures to help keep them nice.

Greg liked to read the scriptures and underline his favorites. Once a week he shared one of his favorite scriptures with his family and helped his younger sister memorize it.

Susan's mom liked to put pictures in scrapbooks to help their family remember the good times.

Bret liked to go to the library and check out good books. He could see that his brother couldn't find some good ones, so he showed him some of his favorites.

Patrick's mom was going to school and she didn't have a place to study. So one day he got an idea and asked his sister help him make a special study spot where it was quiet.

One night Mindy's family decided to camp out in the backyard. Mindy asked them to have a family prayer so they would be safe during the night.

Beth's sister was too young to read or write, so Beth helped her write a special letter to her grandmother.

William really liked to draw, so he made homemade cards and gave them to his family.

Irene was not getting good grades and she was worried, so her brother helped her with her math every night when she got home.

Adam was stuck at school without a ride home, so he called his dad and his dad left work early to rescue him.

Jayson wondered about some of his ancestors who had died and were not yet baptized. He asked his Uncle Dan to help him get the temple work done.

It was time for family home evening, and Jed's mother or father didn't have it ready. Jed rushed into his room to find a story from The *Friend* and read it to his family for the lesson.

Zack liked to have a big breakfast every morning before school, but his Mom needed to sleep in. So he asked her to teach him how, and now Zack cooks breakfast for himself and his brother to let Mom rest.

Ryan helped his little brother take a bath and choose his clothes each Saturday so they could be on time for church every Sunday.

Clara couldn't wait to show her family the new job jar she made. With lots of things to do to help around the house, she made a game out of it so her little brothers and sisters would help.

Lucy loved to give compliments to her family and tell them she loved them.

Ellen had a lot of friends, but when they visited, she included her family in the conversations.

Nate liked to do things with his dad, so he would invite him to go skating or fishing.

Kevin loved his grandfather and called him every day and visited him on the weekends.

Mika liked to be happy. She tried to smile every morning when her mother came in to get her out of bed, even though she was still tired.

BAD-CHOICE WORDSTRIPS TO GLUE ON THE BACKS OF THE RAGGED-EDGED QUILT PIECES:

Justin lied to his mother so his brother wouldn't get in trouble.

One day Clint and his friends were hiking and took his little brother. They left him behind and his little brother wandered off.

Cindy like to gossip and tell her brother's friends things that were not true about him.

When Kayla's brother pushed her off her bike and she skinned her knee, she said she hated him.

Nancy wouldn't listen to her parents when they asked her to do something. One day she was in danger and she didn't listen or obey, and she got hurt.

Megan saw that her sister's friends were being mean to her sister at school. Megan didn't stick up for her or help her because she was afraid of what her friends would think.

Whenever Dana's brother did something good in school or soccer, Dana would never remember to tell him, so he didn't think she noticed.

Valorie liked to say things that hurt her sister's feelings because she thought her sister was her mother's favorite.

Chad could see that his sister was doing bad things and choosing bad friends at school, but he didn't act like he cared.

Mike liked to help his friends with projects from school, but when his sister asked him for help, he said no.

Tisha rode her bike past her brother every day after school, but he would never say hi or care if she got home ok.

Sarah knew her mother needed to get her exercise and wanted to walk with Sarah after school, but Sarah said she was too busy with her friends.

Every Sunday Jenn's grandmother would call them or come over for dinner. Jenn loved her grandmother, but didn't visit much while she was there. This made her grandmother feel lonely and unloved.

Jamie's sister, Heidi, had a pen pal from Switzerland. Heidi wrote her pen pal letters every week. When Jamie brought in the mail she didn't give her sister the letters, so her sister was sad, thinking her pen pal didn't want to write.

In between Primary classes, Derrick raced his friends to the drinking fountain. If he didn't get there first he pushed the others out of the way.

Carson loved to jump on their trampoline. His sister wanted a turn to jump, but Carson kept jumping, making his sister cry.

Anna like to feed her fish and watch them swim to the top for food. One day her brother dumped a bunch of fish food in the bowl and the fish ate too much and died. Anna was so sad.

Linda's mother asked her to set the table for dinner. She said she would and then went off to play. When it was time to eat, the family didn't have plates to eat on or forks to eat with.

Theme 5   Family Members Have Important Responsibilities

BITE-SIZE MEMORIZE

[image of two children] obey UR [father] + [mother] in the Lord, 4 this is [right hand] .

Ephesians 6:1

SCRIPTURE TO MEMORIZE: Memorize the Ephesians 6:1 Bite-size Memorize poster on p. 48 (shown right). Give children a copy of the small Bite-size Memorize on page 49 or print from CD-ROM.*

SONG: Sing "The Family" in the *Children's Songbook*, p. 194. This song is illustrated in *Primary Partners® Singing Fun!—My Family Can Be Forever* book and CD-ROM.

LESSON: Ask, "What important responsibilities do families have?" Answer this question using the scriptures, Primary lessons, and sources below to teach. See Family Responsibilities in *Gospel Principles*, chapter 37.

- Fathers preside, provide, and protect (Proverbs 4:1; *Proclamation*, paragraph 7).
- Mothers nurture their children (Alma 56:47; *"The Family: A Proclamation to the World,"* paragraph 7)
- Children honor and obey their parents and help one another (Exodus 20:12; *Primary 3—CTR B*, lessons 39, 45).
- Extended families lend support when needed (*Proclamation*, paragraph 7).

MORE IDEAS: See More Sharing-Time Activities (Theme 5) previewed in the back of this book, available in the *Primary Partners® Sharing Time Treasures—My Family Can Be Forever* book or CD-ROM (to print images in color or black and white).

Activity: Responsible Family (Upside-Down, Turn-'Em-Around Game)

OBJECTIVE: Tell children, "Our families have responsibilities to help one another. When we don't do what we are supposed to do it makes our family sad. When we do things we are supposed to do without being asked, we make our family happy."

TO MAKE VISUALS: *Copy, color, and cut out four wheels (parts A and B), the four family faces, and the situation cards (p. 50-55). Mount wheel parts A and B together. Laminate wheels and faces separately. Attach a face to each wheel by placing a metal brad (paper fastener) in the nose of each family member and then through the center of the wheel. Tape wheels to a poster, board, or wall. Place situation cards in a container to draw from.

Note: So the brads don't scratch the board or wall, mount the wheels on a poster or tape a 2"x2" paper on the back of each brad.

TO PRESENT: *Note: Before each turn, turn the faces so the heads are pointing left or right, not up or down.* (1) Have children take turns drawing a card, and, without looking at the card, hand it to the leader to read. The leader points to the family member they are to turn, e.g., Mom. (2) Have the child answer the question and then turn the family member's face (mom, dad, sister, or brother) right-side up to show a smile, or upside down to show a frown. (3) Talk about the responsibility for each family member described on the card. (4) If the face is upside down, ask children to tell you how they can "turn 'em around" to make a happy family. Then turn the face around.

[Four circular face wheels labeled "UPSIDE DOWN" and "TURN 'EM AROUND"]

Ephesians 6:1

 , obey UR 🍐 + 🐜🐜 in the Lord, 4 this is 🖐right.

Ephesians 6:1

 , obey UR 🍐 + 🐜🐜 in the Lord, 4 this is 🖐right.

Ephesians 6:1

 , obey UR 🍐 + 🐜🐜 in the Lord, 4 this is 🖐right.

Ephesians 6:1

 , obey UR 🍐 + 🐜🐜 in the Lord, 4 this is 🖐right.

Ephesians 6:1

Make 4 copies.

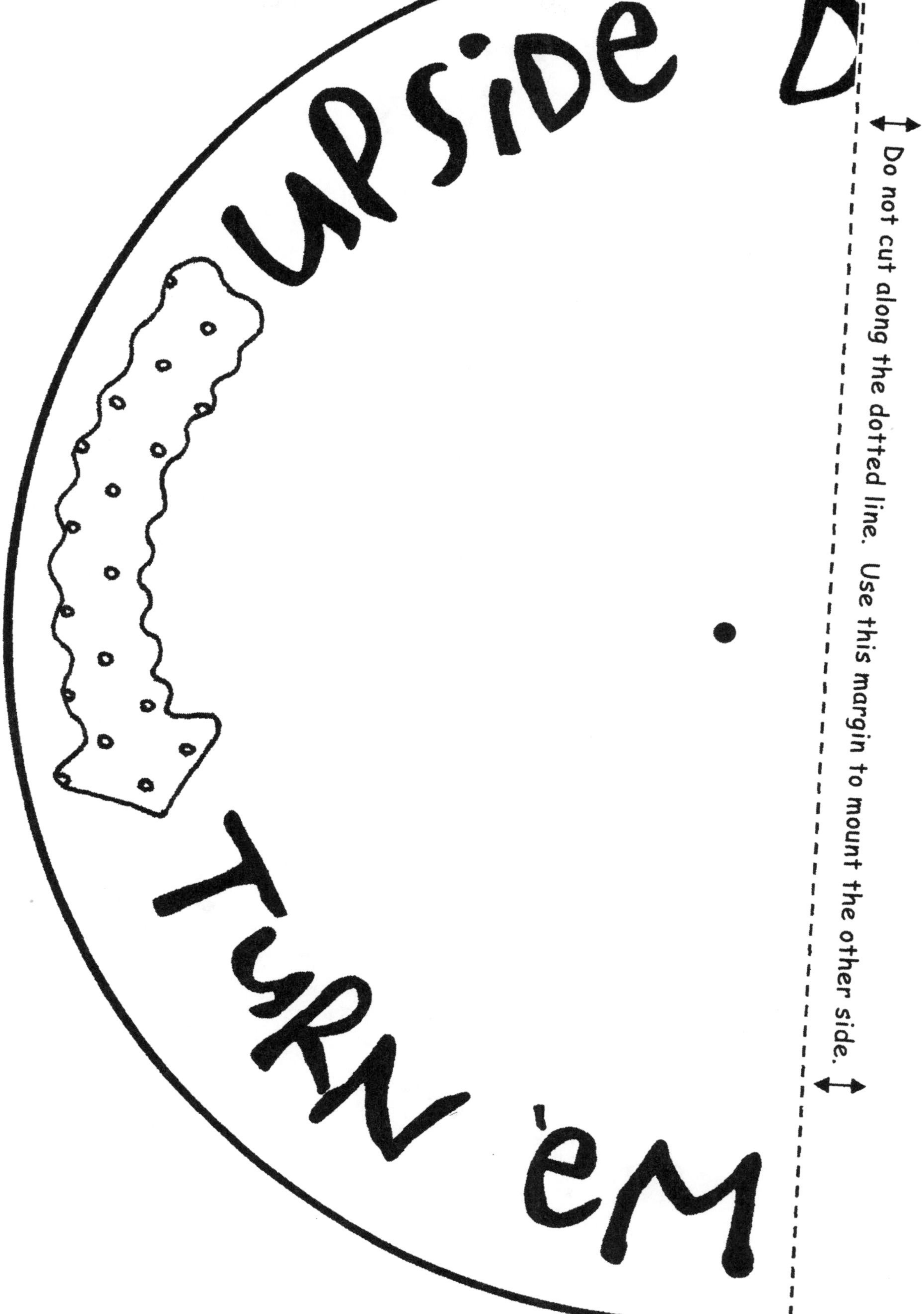

UPSide D

TURN 'eM

Do not cut along the dotted line. Use this margin to mount the other side.

Make 4 copies.

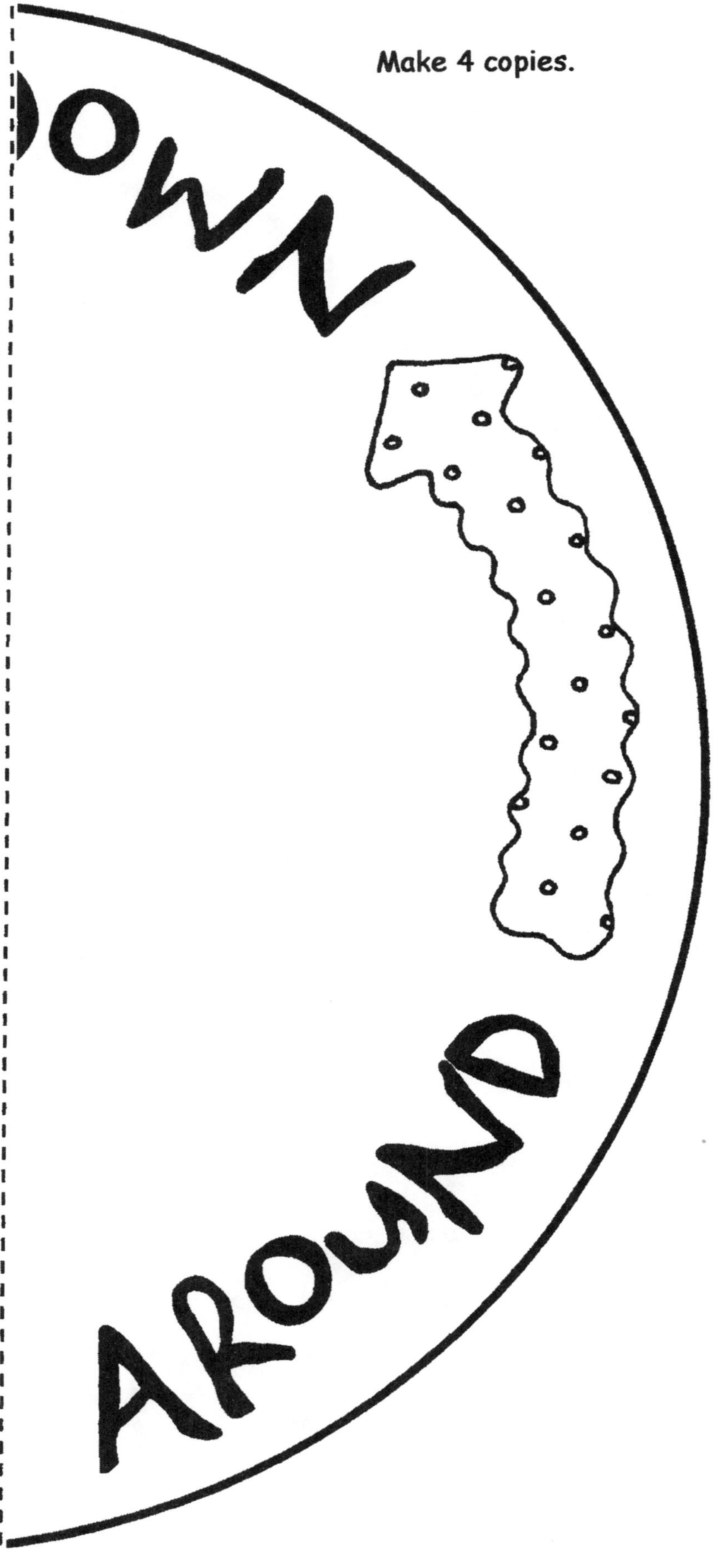

DOWN

Cut carefully along the inside of the dotted line.

AROUND

MOM: Mother asked Carson to bring in the mail and to leave his sister's teddy bear inside. He didn't listen and dropped the bear in the mud while he was getting the mail. Mother didn't scold him, but helped Carson clean the bear.

. . . .

MOM: Jenny's mom came home from the store to find that Jenny had spilled paint all over the living room rug. Her mom yelled at her and sent her to bed without any supper.

. . . .

DAD: Dad asked Jenny to bring her boots home from school each day for a week. Every day she forgot. Dad was upset, but he decided to be kind to Jenny and take her to school to get the boots.

. . . .

DAD: Carson's dad was a coach for the high-school football team and came home from practice every day very tired. Every day, Carson asked him to play ball with him, but his dad never did. This made Carson sad.

. . . .

SISTER: Jenny's baby brother was crying a lot one day and her mom was not feeling well. So Jenny took care of the baby while her mom slept.

. . . .

SISTER: Jenny couldn't wait for Saturday because her mother said she would bake them a strawberry pie from the strawberries in their garden. When Jenny went out to pick them she saw her brother Carson eating the last strawberry. Jenny yelled at her brother and called him names.

. . . .

BROTHER: Jenny was Carson's twin sister. They played together but sometimes didn't get along. One day Carson accidentally pushed Jenny into the rosebush full of thorns. Carson said he was sorry and helped her out and put medicine and bandages on the wounds.

. . . .

BROTHER: Carson's fire engine was his favorite toy until his sister stepped on it and broke a wheel. He felt like yelling at her, but went to his dad instead and asked him to fix it.

. . . .

MOM: Jenny's mother wanted her to read the Book of Mormon every day to build her faith and testimony, and to learn about Nephi and others who obeyed the commandments. Jenny was not reading it, so her mother took the time to read it with her.

MOM: Jenny and her mother were in a hurry to get home and their car got stuck in the mud. Jenny wanted to pray for help, but her mother was too mad to pray and yelled at her daughter.

. . . .

DAD: It was time for Jenny to start school and she asked her father to give her a blessing. This gave her comfort and guided her safely through the school year.

. . . .

DAD: Carson's dad promised to buy him a new pair of shoes when school started. Dad's watch broke and he needed to buy a new one, but he bought Carson's shoes instead.

. . . .

SISTER: Jenny's brother Carson was watching his favorite TV show and it was Jenny's turn to watch the show she liked. Jenny was upset that Carson wouldn't let her watch it. Instead of arguing with him, she decided to watch his show with him and they had a good laugh.

. . . .

SISTER: Jenny went fishing with her brother Carson. After one big catch, Carson told their dad that he caught the two biggest fish, and Jenny knew they were hers. She was so mad that she hit him with the fishing pole and cut his forehead.

. . . .

BROTHER: Carson liked to sleep in every day when it was time to get ready for school. One day Carson was late again, which made his sister Jenny walk into class late again too. This made Jenny's teacher angry, so Jenny started to cry.

. . . .

BROTHER: Carson was asked to sweep the floor really quickly before company came. He was in a hurry to play with his friends, so he swept all the dirt under the rug.

. . . .

MOM: Jenny and her mother bought their groceries and loaded them into the car. Her mother read the receipt and noticed that the grocery man forgot to ring up the eggs. She sent Jenny back in to pay for the eggs. This made Jenny want to be honest.

. . . .

SISTER: Jenny's mother was such a happy mom. She always smiled when Jenny came up to her. One day her mother wasn't smiling and it made Jenny sad. But Jenny wrapped her arms around her mom anyway and told her she loved her.

DAD: Dad was often very tired, but every day he went to work, even when he was sick. He knew it was important to earn enough money to feed and clothe their family and pay their bills.

. . . .

DAD: Dad lost his job and didn't go out to find a new one, so they didn't have enough money to take care of the family.

. . . .

SISTER: Jenny hated to wash the dishes. She didn't like getting her hands into the yucky food that stuck to the plates. One day Jenny asked her mother what to do. Soon they were working together, talking and laughing. She decided that work can be fun, especially when help each other.

. . . .

SISTER: Jenny loved to sneak chocolate chips from the large jar that sat on the panty shelf. Her mother told her not to get into it, but one day she scooped up a bunch just as her mother walked in. Jenny shoved them into her mouth so fast that it made her choke.

. . . .

BROTHER: Carson didn't like to work out in the garden until he thought about what a garden could produce. The tomato plants bring big juicy ripe tomatoes. His dad liked them on sandwiches, his mom like them in salads, and his baby brother liked to squish them between his toes. After knowing what a garden could bring, Carson wanted to weed the tomatoes.

. . . .

MOM: When Jenny had a problem she always went to her mom. Her mom looked her in the eye and listened. She let Jenny talk as long as she wanted. This made Jenny feel like she could tell her mother anything and she would listen.

. . . .

DAD: Carson's dad loved family prayer. He gathered his family around every night and every morning to pray. He said, "Families that pray together stay together." This made Carson feel closer to his family.

. . . .

MOM: Jenny made pancakes for her family every Saturday morning in hopes that her family would say she was a good cook. They scarfed them down and went their way, never saying that they were good. One day her mother said, "Jenny, your pancakes passed the test." This made Jenny happy.

SISTER: Jenny liked to wander off, and one day she walked to the grocery store and her parents didn't know where she was. This made her mother cry and her dad call the police.

. . . .

SISTER: Jenny liked to sing and sometimes she didn't quite know the tunes, but she would sing anyway. One day her dog seemed lonely so she sang to him; she sang to the bird and the bird sang back. One night she sang in family home evening and her family smiled.

. . . .

BROTHER: Carson liked to go to baseball games with his friends—and only his friends. One day he noticed that his younger brother Levi was sad. So he asked Levi to go with them. The game was really fun and Carson wasn't worried about his brother being home alone.

. . . .

BROTHER: Carson couldn't even go into his brother's room because of the mess. His brother couldn't ever find anything with all the clothes and toys scattered everywhere. One day Carson had to help his brother find his soccer uniform, which was hidden under the bed. This is when Carson decided to teach his brother how to clean his room. Now they have a place for everything and his brother can go there to find it.

. . . .

SISTER: Christmas was coming and Jenny wanted every toy that she could see. She made a huge list of things she wanted and rushed it to the mall to drop into the Santa mailbox. She dreamed of all the toys until one day she saw a little girl in her neighborhood who didn't even have a doll. Jenny told her family and they helped Jenny get nice gifts for the little girl.

. . . .

SISTER: Jenny wanted to make friends at school, but the girls she liked were not very nice to her. She told her older sister Kayla. So, Kayla started helping Jenny invite friends over after school. Pretty soon Jenny got to know them and she had all the friends she needed.

Theme 6 — Heavenly Father Teaches Me How to Strengthen My Family

BITE-SIZE MEMORIZE

And ye 🔆 🐝 have a ✋ 2 injure 1 a🐟r, but 2 live peaceably.

Mosiah 4:13

SCRIPTURE TO MEMORIZE: Memorize the Mosiah 4:13 Bite-size Memorize poster on p. 57 (shown right). Give children a copy of the small Bite-size Memorize on page 58 or print from CD-ROM.*

SONG: Sing "Home Can Be a Heaven on Earth" from hymnbook, p. 298. This song is illustrated in *Primary Partners® Singing Fun!—My Family Can Be Forever* book and CD-ROM.

LESSON: Ask, "What things has Heavenly Father taught us to do to strengthen our families?" Answer this question using the scriptures, Primary lessons, and sources below to teach.

- How can family prayer strengthen my family (3 Nephi 18:21; *Primary 1—Nursery*, lesson 27)?
- How can family home evening strengthen my family (3 Nephi 17:3)?
- How can I strengthen my family (Mosiah 18:21)?

MORE IDEAS: See More Sharing-Time Activities (Theme 6) previewed in the back of this book, available in the *Primary Partners® Sharing Time Treasures—My Family Can Be Forever* book or CD-ROM (images in color or black and white).

Activity: My Family Can Be Happy ("Be a Happy Camper" Backpack Decisions)

OBJECTIVE: Say to children, "Let's pretend that this life on earth with our families is a camping trip. If you want your family to be happy campers, to enjoy their time on earth as a family, what would you pack? Let's pack only things that will strengthen our family and leave behind items that would weaken our family."

TO MAKE VISUALS: *Copy, color, cut out, and laminate the *Happy Camper* and *Sad Camper* backpacks and objects (p. 59-67). Post backpacks on the board or wall and place objects in a container to draw from.

TO PRESENT:

1. Have children take turns choosing an object, reading it aloud, and taping it on the correct backpack.
2. Talk about each item and how the action will help your family to be a *Happy Camper* or a *Sad Camper*.
3. If you want to compete, you can divide into teams and award a point for each *Happy Camper* item drawn.
4. When you are finished packing the *Sad Camper* backpack, tell children that you are going to toss this backpack away. These are things you will not take with you. Review these if there is time, and have the children actually put each one of these in the trash.

*All images can be printed in full color and black and white using the CD-ROM: *Primary Partners Sharing Time—My Family Can Be Forever.*

And ye ⊕ have a MIND 2 injure 1 a + 🥜 + r, but 2 live peaceably.

Mosiah 4:13

And ye  have a 2 injure 1 a+🥜+r, but 2 live peaceably.

Mosiah 4:13

And ye have a 2 injure 1 a+🥜+r, but 2 live peaceably.

Mosiah 4:13

And ye 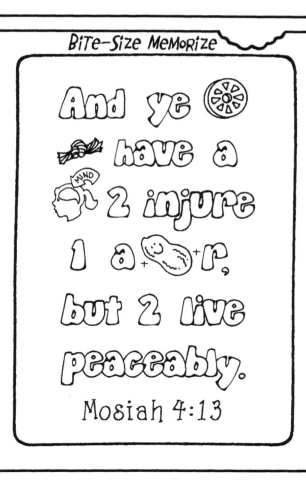 have a 2 injure 1 a+🥜+r, but 2 live peaceably.

Mosiah 4:13

And ye 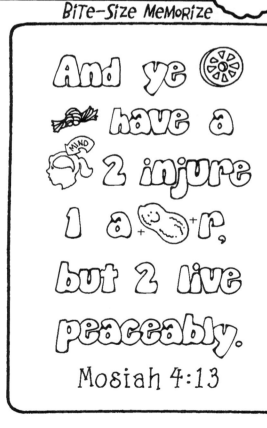 have a 2 injure 1 a+🥜+r, but 2 live peaceably.

Mosiah 4:13

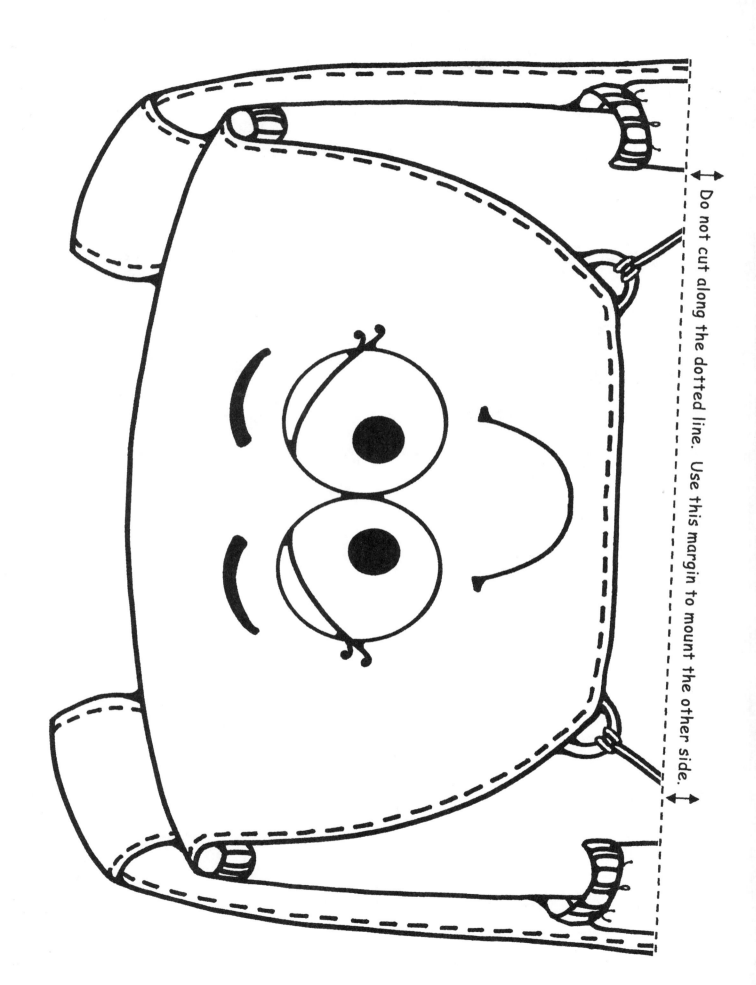

Do not cut along the dotted line. Use this margin to mount the other side.

Cut carefully along the inside of the dotted line.

HAPPY CAMPER

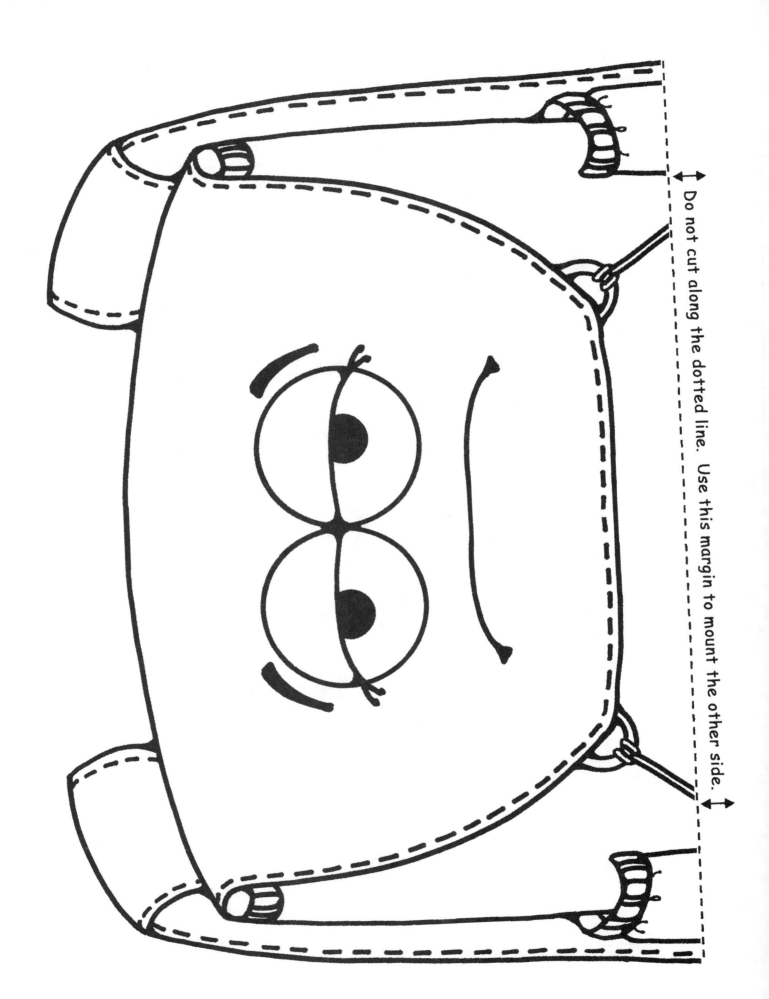

Do not cut along the dotted line. Use this margin to mount the other side.

Cut carefully along the inside of the dotted line.

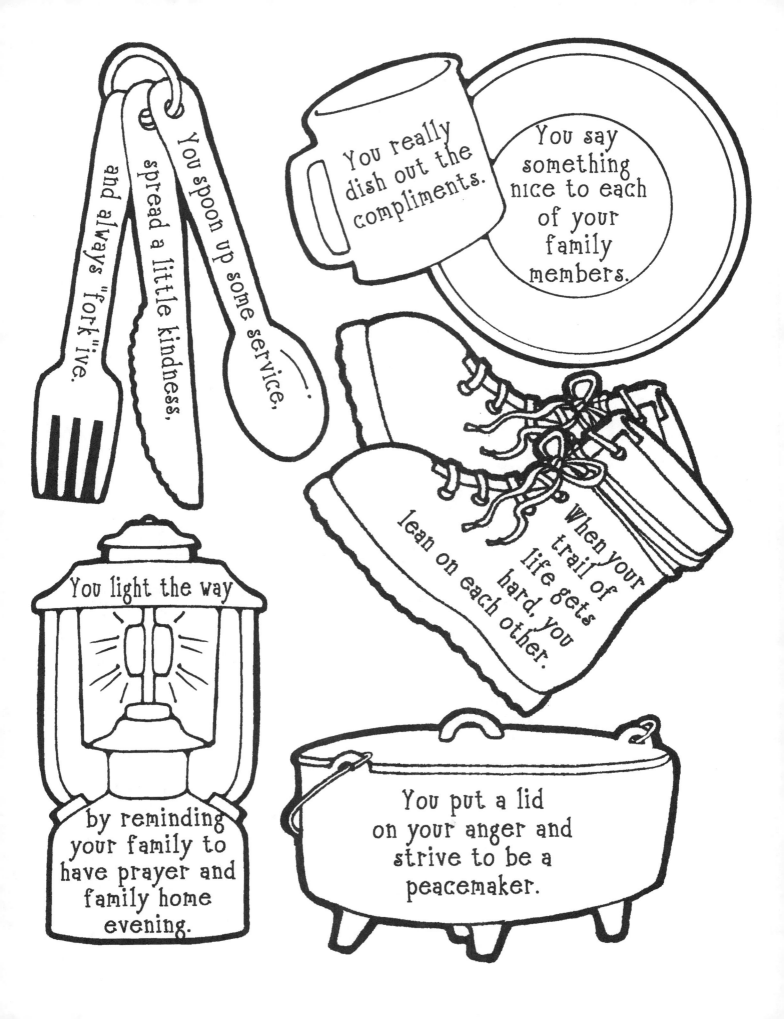

and always "fork"ive.

spread a little kindness,

You spoon up some service,

You really dish out the compliments.

You say something nice to each of your family members.

When your trail of life gets hard, you lean on each other.

You light the way by reminding your family to have prayer and family home evening.

You put a lid on your anger and strive to be a peacemaker.

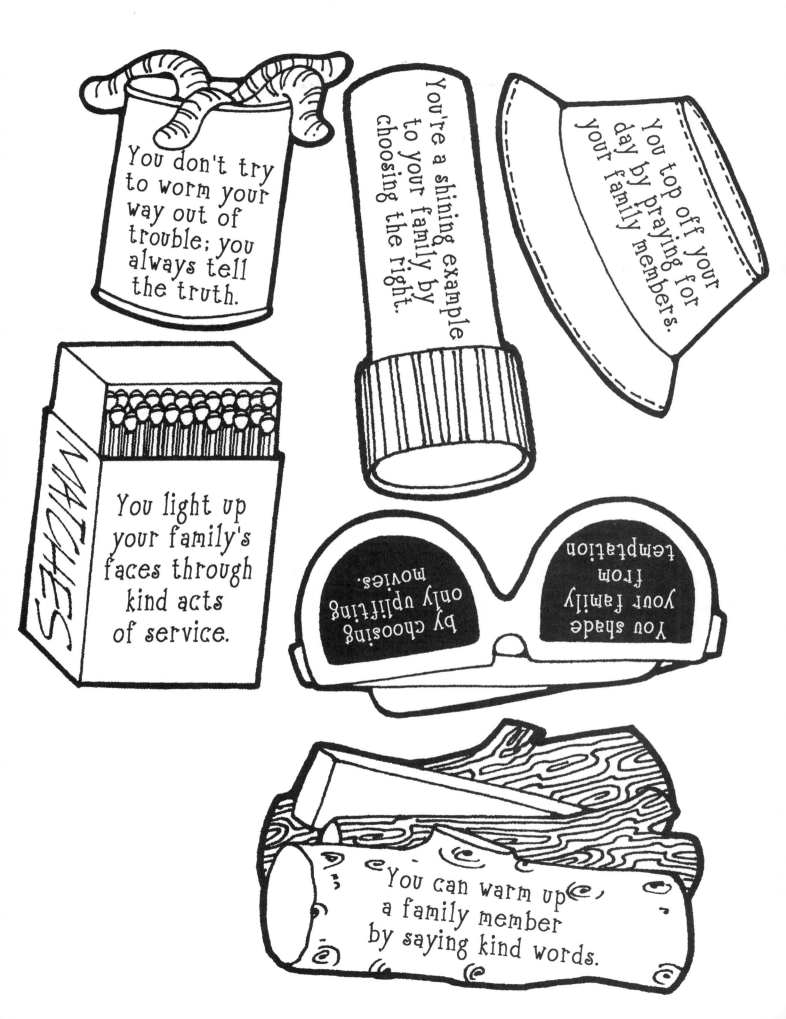

You don't try to worm your way out of trouble; you always tell the truth.

You're a shining example to your family by choosing the right.

You top off your day by praying for your family members.

You light up your family's faces through kind acts of service.

MATCHES

You shade your family from temptation by choosing only uplifting movies.

You can warm up a family member by saying kind words.

You put your arms around a family member and let them know of your love.

When a family member is sad, you are a rainy-day friend by listening and caring.

BUG SPRAY

You don't bug your mom by whining and complaining.

You get enough sleep so you will be strong enough to help and not be grumpy.

You take care of your home to make it a pleasant place to live.

You go fishing for great family home evening ideas and you enjoy your time together.

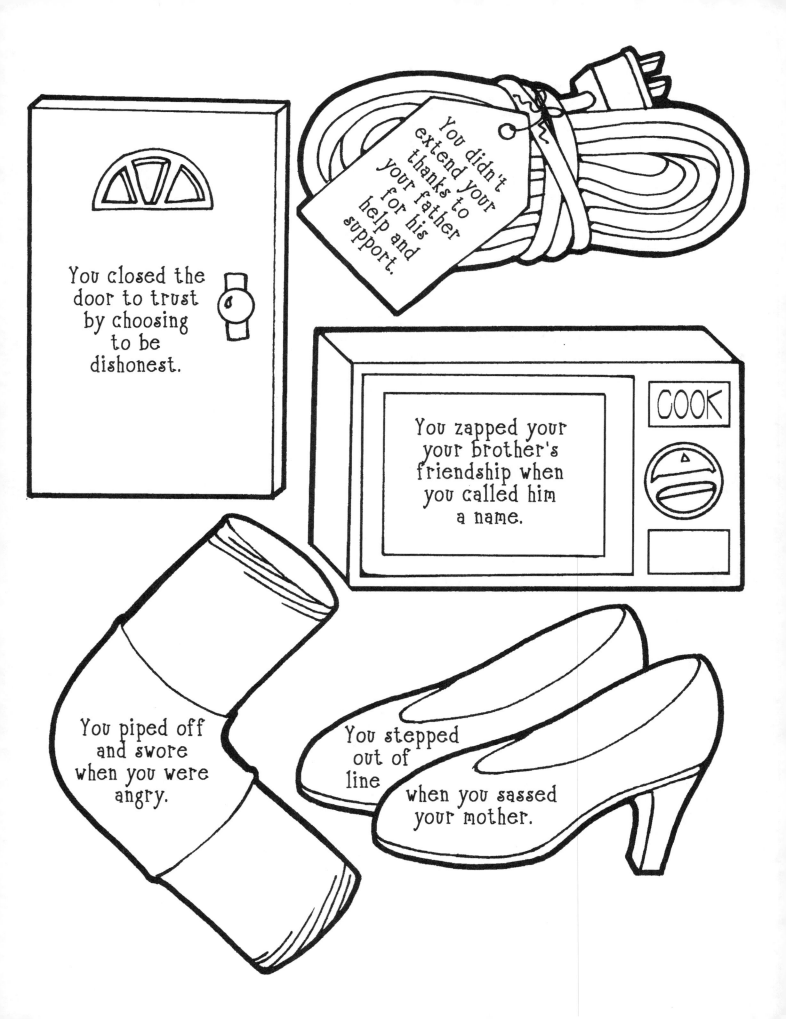

You closed the door to trust by choosing to be dishonest.

You didn't extend your thanks to your father for his help and support.

You zapped your your brother's friendship when you called him a name.

COOK

You piped off and swore when you were angry.

You stepped out of line when you sassed your mother.

Theme 7   Temples Unite Families

Let this 🏠
🐝 built N2
m👁 name,
t👂👁 may
reveal m👁•n
⚡dinances
therein N2
m👁 👨‍👩‍👧.
  people

D&C 124:40

SCRIPTURE TO MEMORIZE: Memorize the D&C 124:40 Bite-size Memorize poster on p. 69 (shown right). Give children a copy of the small Bite-size Memorize on page 70 or print from CD-ROM.*

SONG: Sing "Families Can Be Together Forever" in the *Children's Songbook*, p. 188. This song is illustrated in *Primary Partners® Singing Fun!—My Family Can Be Forever* book and CD-ROM.

LESSON: Ask, "How do temples unite our families?" Answer this question using the scriptures, Primary lessons, and sources below to teach.

- Being baptized and keeping my baptismal covenants can help me prepare to receive the blessings of the temple (3 Nephi 11:33; Mosiah 18:8-10; *Primary 3—CTR B*, lessons 11, 13).
- Being temple worthy now can bless me and my family (Alma 34:32; 37:35).
- My family can be together forever through the covenants and ordinances of the temple (D&C 138:47-48; *Primary 3—CTR B*, lesson 35).
- Family history work and temple work unite the generations of my family and help me remember my heritage (Malachi 4:5-6; *Primary 5—D&C*, lesson 34; *Gospel Principles*, chapter 40).

MORE IDEAS: See More Sharing-Time Activities (Theme 7) previewed in the back of this book, available in the *Primary Partners® Sharing Time Treasures—My Family Can Be Forever* book or CD-ROM (to print images in color or black and white).

Activity: Temples Strengthen Our Family Ties
Heart-to-Heart Family-Tie Quiz)

OBJECTIVE: Ask children, "How do temples strengthen our family ties, holding families together forever? Let's take a *Heart-to-Heart Family-Tie Quiz* to learn how.

TO MAKE VISUALS: (1) *Copy, color, and cut out the quiz questions and dolls (p. 71-76). You'll need a doll for every question you plan to use. (2) Tape a quiz question on the back of each doll. (3) Paper punch hands, and place page reinforcers in the back of each. Or, before punching, place a piece of tape behind each hand to reinforce. (4) You'll need tape and a narrow 7" ribbon or piece of yarn for each doll.

TO PRESENT:

1. Begin by taping the temple to the board, then read the sign "Temples Strengthen Our Family Ties."

2. Have children come up one at a time, choose a doll, and hand the question to the leader to read.

3. The child tries to answer the question. If they can't their class can help. If not, anyone can answer. The answers are written next to the question.

4. After the question is answered, tape the doll to the wall and tie a string and a bow from one doll to the next, connecting the hearts and hands to symbolize that temples unite families.

Let this 🏠 built N2 m+👁 name, t+🎩👁 may reveal m+👁+n /+dinances therein N2 m+👁 people.

D&C 124:40

Let this 🏠 🐝 built N2 m+👁 name, t+👒 👁 may reveal m👁+n /+dinances therein N2 m+👁 people.

D&C 124:40

Let this 🏠 🐝 built N2 m+👁 name, t+👒 👁 may reveal m👁+n /+dinances therein N2 m+👁 people.

D&C 124:40

Let this 🏠 🐝 built N2 m+👁 name, t+👒 👁 may reveal m👁+n /+dinances therein N2 m+👁 people.

D&C 124:40

Let this 🏠 🐝 built N2 m+👁 name, t+👒 👁 may reveal m👁+n /+dinances therein N2 m+👁 people.

D&C 124:40

QUIZ: HOW DO TEMPLES UNITE FAMILIES SO THEY CAN BE TOGETHER FOREVER?
CHOOSE THE ONES THAT BEST SUIT YOUR CHILDREN

IF SOMEONE DIES BEFORE BEING BAPTIZED, HOW CAN HE RECEIVE THIS SPECIAL ORDINANCE?
(A person can go to the temple and be baptized.)

HOW DOES PAYING OUR TITHING HELP TEMPLE WORK?
(To build temples so the work can be done.)

ONCE A FAMILY IS SEALED TOGETHER, IS THAT ALL THEY HAVE TO DO TO BE TOGETHER FOREVER?
(No, families must continue to keep the commandments.)

WHAT DO WE HAVE TO DO SO WE CAN GO TO THE TEMPLE AND BE BAPTIZED FOR THE DEAD?
(Be a member at least 12 years old and obtain a temple recommend from the bishop.)

WHAT IS A TEMPLE RECOMMEND?
(A document given to a worthy member that allows them to enter into the temple and perform work there.)

WHEN WE DIE, CAN WE LIVE AGAIN WITH OUR FAMILIES IN HEAVEN?
(Yes, if we are sealed in the temple before we die, or someone does the work for us after we die.)

WHAT DO WE LEARN ABOUT IN THE TEMPLES?
(About Heavenly Father's plan of salvation for us.)

WHAT DO YOU LEARN WHEN YOU GO TO THE TEMPLE?
(What you need to do so that you can return to live with Heavenly Father.)

WHAT DO YOU NEED TO DO TO GET A TEMPLE RECOMMEND?
(Be at lease 12 years of age and keep the commandments. Adults can obtain a different recommend to do work in addition to baptisms.)

WHO CAN GIVE YOU A TEMPLE RECOMMEND?
(The bishop or his counselors.)

BEFORE YOU GO TO THE TEMPLE, HOW SHOULD YOU FEEL ABOUT HEAVENLY FATHER AND JESUS?
(Have a testimony of Their gospel, love Them, and have a desire to keep Their commandments.)

WHAT ARE SOME WAYS WE CAN PREPARE FOR THE TEMPLE?
(Attend sacrament meeting, pay tithing, keep the Word of Wisdom, be kind to others, obey parents, and keep the commandments.)

HOW IS IT POSSIBLE THAT WE CAN LIVE FOREVER?
(Because Jesus died for us and was resurrected so we might live again.)

WHY DOES HEAVENLY FATHER WANT ALL FAMILIES TO BE SEALED IN THE TEMPLE?
(So we can be happy and be part of His eternal family.)

IF A PERSON DIES WITHOUT HEARING THE GOSPEL, HOW WILL HE LEARN THE GOSPEL?
(Through the missionaries who will teach him in the spirit world.)

WHAT MUST WE DO IN ORDER TO RETURN TO LIVE WITH HEAVENLY FATHER?
(Be baptized and receive temple ordinances so we can live in God's kingdom.)

BY WHAT POWER ARE TEMPLE ORDINANCES PERFORMED?
(By the power of the priesthood.)

WHAT DOES IT MEAN WHEN A MAN AND A WOMAN ARE SEALED TOGETHER FOR TIME AND ETERNITY IN THE TEMPLE?
(They will be husband and wife on this earth and after they die.)

IF YOUR PARENTS WERE SEALED IN THE TEMPLE BEFORE YOU WERE BORN, DO YOU NEED TO GO TO THE TEMPLE AND BE SEALED TO THEM?
(No, because you are born in the covenant of their eternal marriage.)

WHAT ARE SOME OF THE ORDINANCES IN THE TEMPLE?
(Baptism for the dead, temple marriage, sealing of families together forever.)

WHAT IF OUR PARENTS ARE NOT MARRIED IN THE TEMPLE, HOW CAN WE BECOME AN ETERNAL FAMILY?
(Parents can first be sealed in the temple, and then have their children sealed to them.)

HOW CAN YOU HAVE YOUR ANCESTORS BAPTIZED AND SEALED TO THEIR FAMILIES?
(Searching family histories, records, and journals. Then submit their names to the temple to have the work done.)

WHY IS OBEYING THE WORD OF WISDOM IMPORTANT TO PREPARE US FOR THE TEMPLE?
(Our body is a temple in which our spirit lives. We must keep our body clean so that it (body and spirit) can enter the temple.)

WHY IS IT IMPORTANT TO LIVE THE COMMANDMENTS EVEN AFTER WE ARE SEALED IN THE TEMPLE?
(So we can be worthy to live with Heavenly Father and Jesus and family members who are righteous.)

WHAT DOES IT MEAN TO BE SEALED TOGETHER FOREVER?
(Families won't be separated when they die, they can live together always.)

Theme 8   Faith, Prayer, Repentance, and Forgiveness
              Can Strengthen My Family

SCRIPTURE TO MEMORIZE: Memorize *"The Family: A Proclamation to the World "* Bite-size Memorize poster on p. 78 (shown right). Give children a copy of the small Bite-size Memorize on page 79 or print from CD-ROM.*

SONG: Sing "I Pray in Faith" in the *Children's Songbook*, p. 14. This song is illustrated in *Primary Partners® Singing Fun!—My Family Can Be Forever* book and CD-ROM.

LESSON: Ask, "How can faith, prayer, repentance, and forgiveness help strengthen my family?" Answer this question using the scriptures, Primary lessons, and sources below to teach.

• Faith in the Lord strengthens me and my family (Alma 32:21; D&C 6:36; 8:10; *Primary 3—CTR B*, lesson 7).

• Prayer strengthens me and my family (D&C 68:28; *Primary 3—CTR B*, lesson 19).

• Repentance returns me to the Lord's plan (D&C 58:42-43; *Primary 1—Nursery*, lesson 29; *Primary 3—CTR B*, lesson 10).

• To be forgiven, I must forgive (D&C 64:9-10; *Primary 3—CTR B*, lesson 23).

MORE IDEAS: See More Sharing-Time Activities (Theme 8) previewed in the back of this book, available in the *Primary Partners® Sharing Time Treasures—My Family Can Be Forever* book or CD-ROM (to print images in color or black and white).

Activity: My Smooth-Sailing Family (Lovey's-Landing S.O.S. Game)

OBJECTIVE: Tell children, that their family, like the Lovey family, can learn to love one another and get through the rough waters or storms of life. We can do this by solving our problems through parking our boats at the right docks: Faith, Prayer, Repentance, or Forgiveness."

TO MAKE VISUALS: *Copy, color, and cut out visuals (p. 80-85). Put boat dock together. Then laminate boat dock and boats and cut out boats. Place boats in a container to draw from. Have double-stick tape ready to mount boats on docks.

TO PRESENT: (1) Divide players into two teams and have teams take turns drawing a boat from the container and reading it aloud. (2) The player's team can help them decide the best solution to the problem and move their boat to that dock/solution: Faith, Prayer, Repentance, or Forgiveness. Then tell how this can solve the problem. Use double-stick tape to mount boats near docks. (3) If they land at the right dock they earn a point for their team. If not, the other team has a chance to answer by moving their boat to the right dock. After all are answered, the team with the most points wins!

*All images can be printed in full color and black and white using the CD-ROM: *Primary Partners Sharing Time—My Family Can Be Forever.*

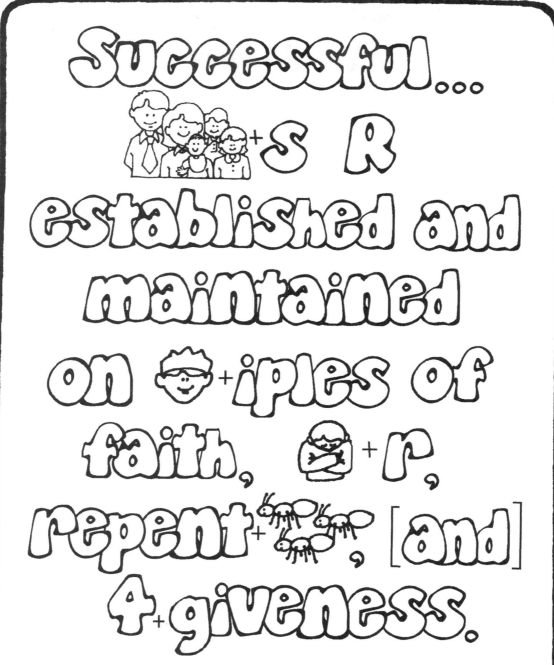

Successful... family+S R established and maintained on child+iples of faith, prayer+r, repent+ants, [and] 4+giveness.

The Family: A Proclamation to the World
Paragraph 7

Successful...
👨‍👩‍👧‍👦 + s R established and maintained on 😎 + iples of faith, 🙏 + r, repent + 🐜, [and] 4 + giveness. 

The Family: A Proclamation
to the World
Paragraph 7

Bite-Size Memorize

Successful...
👨‍👩‍👧‍👦 + s R established and maintained on 😎 + iples of faith, 🙏 + r, repent + 🐜, [and] 4 + giveness. 

The Family: A Proclamation
to the World
Paragraph 7

Bite-Size Memorize

Successful...
👨‍👩‍👧‍👦 + s R established and maintained on 😎 + iples of faith, 🙏 + r, repent + 🐜, [and] 4 + giveness. 

The Family: A Proclamation
to the World
Paragraph 7

Bite-Size Memorize

Successful...
👨‍👩‍👧‍👦 + s R established and maintained on 😎 + iples of faith, 🙏 + r, repent + 🐜, [and] 4 + giveness. 

The Family: A Proclamation
to the World
Paragraph 7

Faith

Do not cut along the dotted line. Use this margin to mount the other side.

Cut carefully along the inside of the dotted line.

Do not cut along the dotted line. Use this margin to mount the other side.

Prayer

Lovey's

Repentance

Landing

Cut carefully along the inside of the dotted line.

Do not cut along the dotted line. Use this margin to mount the other side.

Cut carefully along the inside of the dotted line.

Forgiveness

The Lovey family prayed that they would be protected on their trip. What should they do?

Lacey learned about Jesus Christ in family home evening. She prayed to have a testimony of Him. What should she do?

Landon Lovey had a special mitt grandpa gave him, but Lewis left it outside and it got ruined. What should Landon do?

Landon Lovey was teasing Lewis and making him cry. What should Landon do?

Mother Lovey worked for days making Lacey a new dress, but Lacey didn't even thank her. What should Lacey do?

The Lovey family went camping and Lewis wandered off. What should they do?

Landon Lovey was tempted to make a wrong choice. He needed some extra help. What should he do?

The Lovey family needed to move for Father's new job. They needed help to find a new home. What should they do?

Father Lovey asked Lewis why he was late. Lewis told his father a lie. What should Lewis do?

The Lovey children were worried about their dog, who was missing. What should they do?

Theme 9 Respect, Love, Work, and Wholesome Recreation Can Strengthen My Family

BiTe-SiZe MeMoRiZe

Successful... [families] R established and maintained on [princi]ples of... respect, (Love), compassion, work, and wholesome recreational activities.

The Family: A Proclamation to the World
Paragraph 7

SCRIPTURE TO MEMORIZE: Memorize *"The Family: A Proclamation to the World "* Bite-size Memorize poster on p. 87 (shown right). Give children a copy of the small Bite-size Memorize on page 88 or print from CD-ROM.*

LESSON: Ask, "How can respect, love, work, and wholesome recreation strengthen your family?" Answer this question using the scriptures, Primary lessons, and sources below to teach.

- Showing respect for each other strengthens my family (Matthew 7:12).
- Showing love and compassion strengthens my family (John 13:34-35; Luke 10:33).
- Working together strengthens my family (Exodus 20:9; *Gospel Principles*, chapter 27).
- Participating in wholesome recreational activities helps my family develop unity and love for one another (*Gospel Principles*, chapter 27; *Proclamation*, paragraph 7).

MORE IDEAS: See More Sharing-Time Activities (Theme 9) previewed in the back of this book, available in the *Primary Partners® Sharing Time Treasures—My Family Can Be Forever* book or CD-ROM (to print images in color or black and white).

Activity: Building a Strong Family (Home-"Tweet"-Home Building Project)

OBJECTIVE: Tell children, "Birds of a feather stick together. This means that families that love and respect each other, work together, and participate in wholesome activities, can make their home a sweet ('tweet') place to be. Let's learn how we can build a strong home (or birdhouse) where our family can be happy."

TO MAKE VISUALS: *Copy, color, and cut out the birdhouse and bird cards (p. 89-95). Put together birdhouse according to directions. Sit the birdhouse high so that the opening is within reach of the children. Place the bird cards in a container to draw from. Have tape ready to tape cards to the board or wall. You'll need a piece of straw or raffia string for every child.

TO PRESENT:

1. Give every child a piece of straw or a 6-inch piece of raffia to place in the birdhouse.

2. Have children take turns choosing a bird card and reading it aloud. Then tell how they can help build a strong family by helping in this situation, e.g., "Grandma needs an operation."

3. Tape the bird card on the wall next to the birdhouse.

4. Then place a piece of straw (or raffia) into the opening of the birdhouse to symbolize your comment (promise) to help strengthen your family.

*All images can be printed in full color and black and white using the CD-ROM:
Primary Partners Sharing Time—My Family Can Be Forever.*

Successful...

[family] + S R established and maintained on [principles] of... respect, [Love], compassion, work, and wholesome recreational activities.

The Family: A Proclamation
to the World
Paragraph 7

Successful... [family] +s R established and maintained on [head]+iples of... respect, [Love], compassion, work, and wholesome recreational activities.

The Family: A Proclamation to the World
Paragraph 7

Successful... [family] +s R established and maintained on [head]+iples of... respect, [Love], compassion, work, and wholesome recreational activities.

The Family: A Proclamation to the World
Paragraph 7

Successful... [family] +s R established and maintained on [head]+iples of... respect, [Love], compassion, work, and wholesome recreational activities.

The Family: A Proclamation to the World
Paragraph 7

Successful... [family] +s R established and maintained on [head]+iples of... respect, [Love], compassion, work, and wholesome recreational activities.

The Family: A Proclamation to the World
Paragraph 7

Fold back and glue to roof.

Fold back and glue to roof.

Fold back and glue to side.

Fold back and glue to side.

Fold back and glue to base.

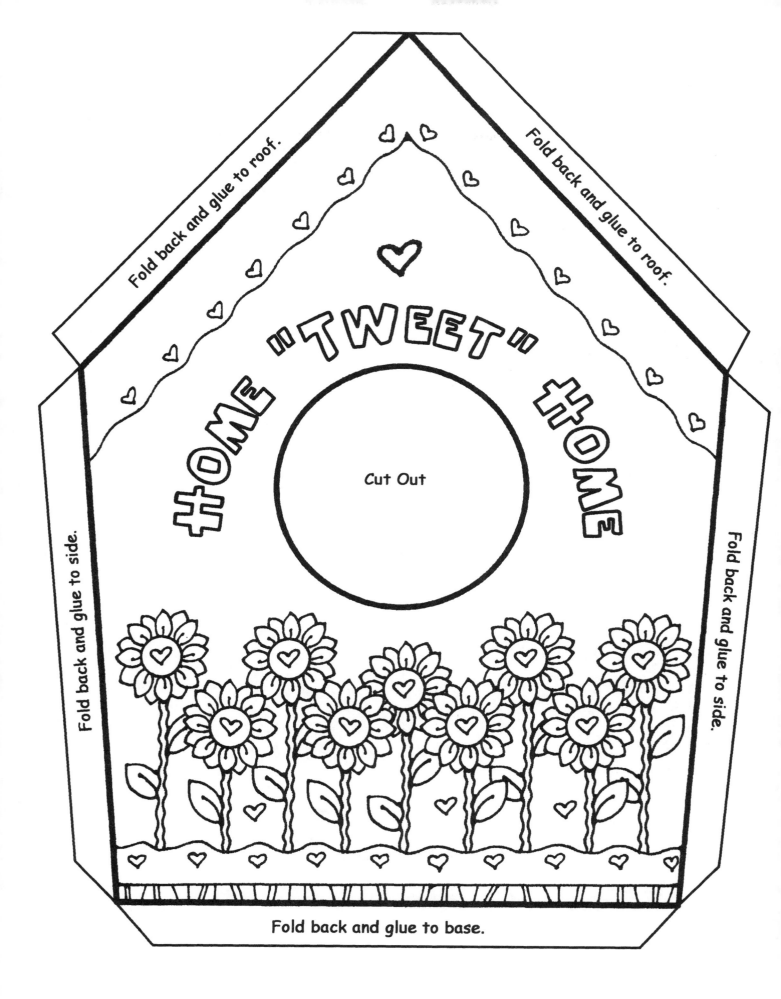

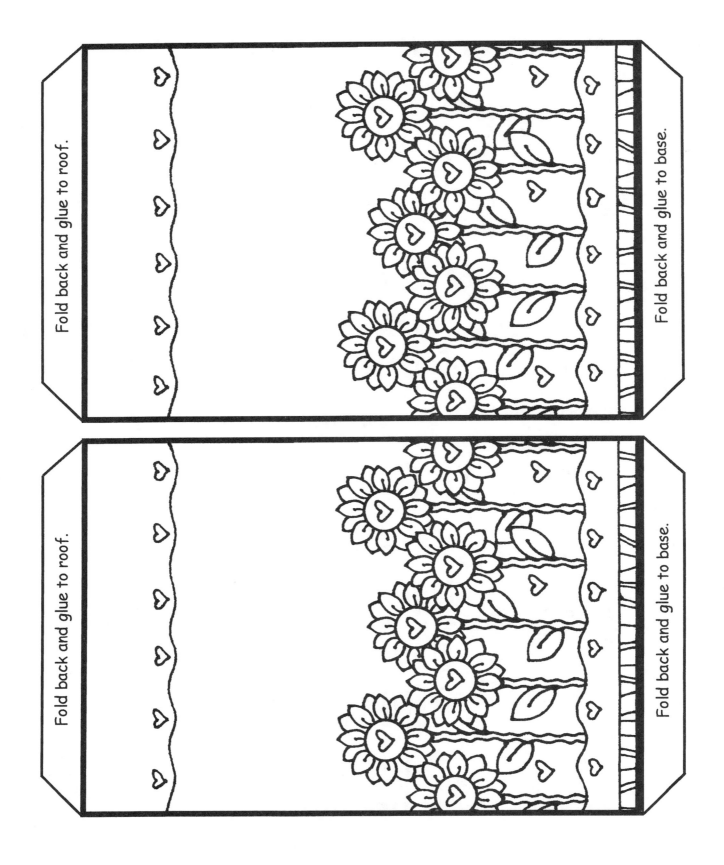

Fold back and glue to roof.

Fold back and glue to base.

Fold back and glue to roof.

Fold back and glue to base.

Fold and glue to tab on other side of roof.

Fold and glue to tab on other side of roof.

Birdhouse Base

Brother and sister have their own daily chores to do.

It was your family's turn to help clean the church.

Grandma has a hard time keeping up her yard.

Brother loves to play board games after school.

Brother needed to learn to swim to earn his merit badge.

Sister felt sad because her best friend moved away.

Father loves to go fishing as often as he can.

Mother asked me to come in for dinner.

Grandpa lives far away and misses his grandchildren.

Mother was not feeling well and the house was a mess.

Theme 10   Prophets Teach Me How to Strengthen My Family

SCRIPTURE TO MEMORIZE: Memorize the D&C 1:38 Bite-size Memorize poster on p. 97 (shown right). Give children a copy of the small Bite-size Memorize on page 98 or print from CD-ROM.*

LESSON: Ask, "What do the prophets teach us that will strengthen our family?" Answer this question using the scriptures, Primary lessons, and sources below to teach.

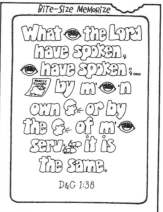

Bite-Size Memorize

What [eye] the Lord have spoken, [eye] have spoken;... [scriptures] by m[eye] [in] own [voice] or by the [voice] of m[eye] [eye] serv[heart] it is the same.

D&C 1:38

- Bible prophets teach me how to strengthen my family (Deuteronomy 6:4-7; Exodus 20:12).
- Book of Mormon prophets teach me how to strengthen my family (Mosiah 27; Mosiah 4:14-15).
- Latter-day prophets teach me how to strengthen my family (select teachings that meet the needs of the children; see general conference issues [May and Nov.] of the *Ensign* and the "Come Listen to a Prophet's Voice" section of the *Friend*).
- The prophet today teaches me how to strengthen my family.

MORE IDEAS: See More Sharing-Time Activities (Theme 10) previewed in the back of this book, available in the *Primary Partners® Sharing Time Treasures—My Family Can Be Forever* book or CD-ROM (to print images in color or black and white).

Activity: The Prophet's Words Strengthen My Family
(Following-the-Prophet-Strengthens-My-Family Match Game)

Following the Prophet Strengthens My Family

Family Life Can Be Sweet As We Live the Gospel

Sandwich In Some Family Time To Be Together

Your Family Is One In a "Melon" So Treat Them Right

Family Service Is a Piece of Cake

OBJECTIVE: Tell children, "Following the prophet will help strengthen your family. Let's learn about what the prophets from the Bible, Book of Mormon, and the latter days have said to make our family strong and happy."

TO MAKE VISUALS: *Copy, color, and cut out the family picnic sign, food signs, and matching food-puzzle pieces (p. 99-108).

TO PRESENT: (1) Mount on the board the "Following the Prophet Strengthens My Family" sign in the center of the board or wall and talk about it. (2) Have four children come up, read, and post the four large signs (melon, corn, cake, and sandwich) as shown right on the board, e.g., post the melon sign: "You're family is one in a melon (million) so treat them right." (3) Divide the matching pieces in half and place on the wall or side of the board faceup with double-stick tape. (4) Have children take turns coming up and choosing a match to the prophet's message. When a match is made, read it aloud and post it under the matching food sign. Talk about each and how it can make family life happy.

*All images can be printed in full color and black and white using the CD-ROM:
Primary Partners Sharing Time—My Family Can Be Forever.

What I the Lord have spoken, I have spoken;... by mine own voice or by the voice of my servants, it is the same.

D&C 1:38

Bite-Size Memorize

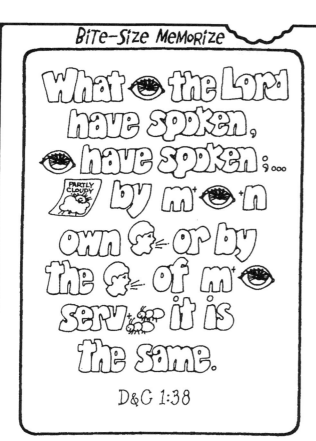

What 👁 the Lord have spoken, 👁 have spoken;... by m+👁+n own ⚡ or by the ⚡ of m+👁 serv🐜 it is the same.

D&C 1:38

Bite-Size Memorize

What 👁 the Lord have spoken, 👁 have spoken;... by m+👁+n own ⚡ or by the ⚡ of m+👁 serv🐜 it is the same.

D&C 1:38

Bite-Size Memorize

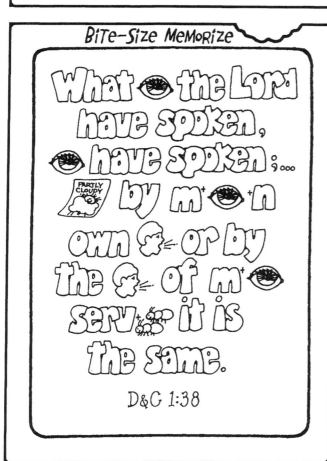

What 👁 the Lord have spoken, 👁 have spoken;... by m+👁+n own ⚡ or by the ⚡ of m+👁 serv🐜 it is the same.

D&C 1:38

Bite-Size Memorize

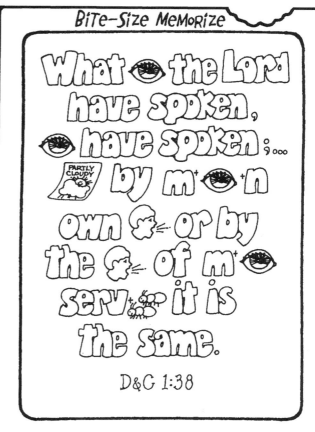

What 👁 the Lord have spoken, 👁 have spoken;... by m+👁+n own ⚡ or by the ⚡ of m+👁 serv🐜 it is the same.

D&C 1:38

Following the Prophet

Do not cut along the dotted line. Use this margin to mount the other side.

Cut carefully along the inside of the dotted line.

Strengthens My Family

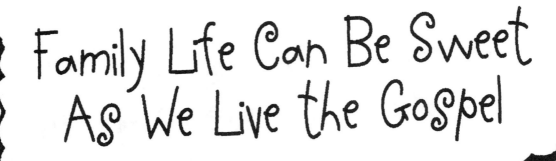

Family Life Can Be Sweet
As We Live the Gospel

Sandwich In Some
Family Time To
Be Together

Is a Piece
of Cake

Family Service

Your
Family
Is
"One In
a
"Melon"
So Treat
Them Right

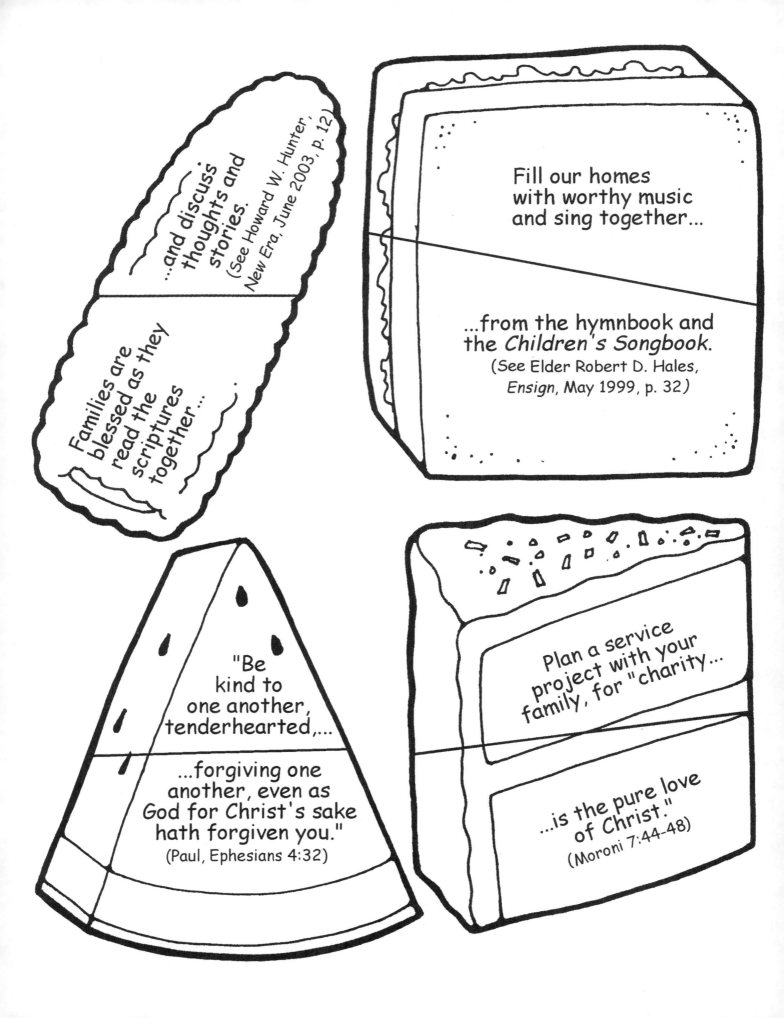

...and discuss thoughts and stories. (See Howard W. Hunter, New Era, June 2003, p. 12)

Families are blessed as they read the scriptures together...

Fill our homes with worthy music and sing together...

...from the hymnbook and the *Children's Songbook*. (See Elder Robert D. Hales, *Ensign*, May 1999, p. 32)

"Be kind to one another, tenderhearted,...

...forgiving one another, even as God for Christ's sake hath forgiven you." (Paul, Ephesians 4:32)

Plan a service project with your family, for "charity...

...is the pure love of Christ." (Moroni 7:44-48)

...will provide a fertile seedbed for a testimony to grow." (Thomas S. Monson, Ensign, Oct. 2001, p. 3)

"A love for the Savior, a reverence for His name, and genuine respect one for another...

Work together as a family...

...and talk to each other as you work. (See Elder Robert D. Hales, Ensign, May 1999, p. 32)

"When you raise your voice in anger...

...the Spirit departs from your home." (Harold B. Lee, Ensign, May 1999, p. 32)

Be caring and helpful to the poor, the sick, and the needy,...

...assisting the widows and the fatherless. (See Ezra Taft Benson, Ensign, August 1993, p. 2)

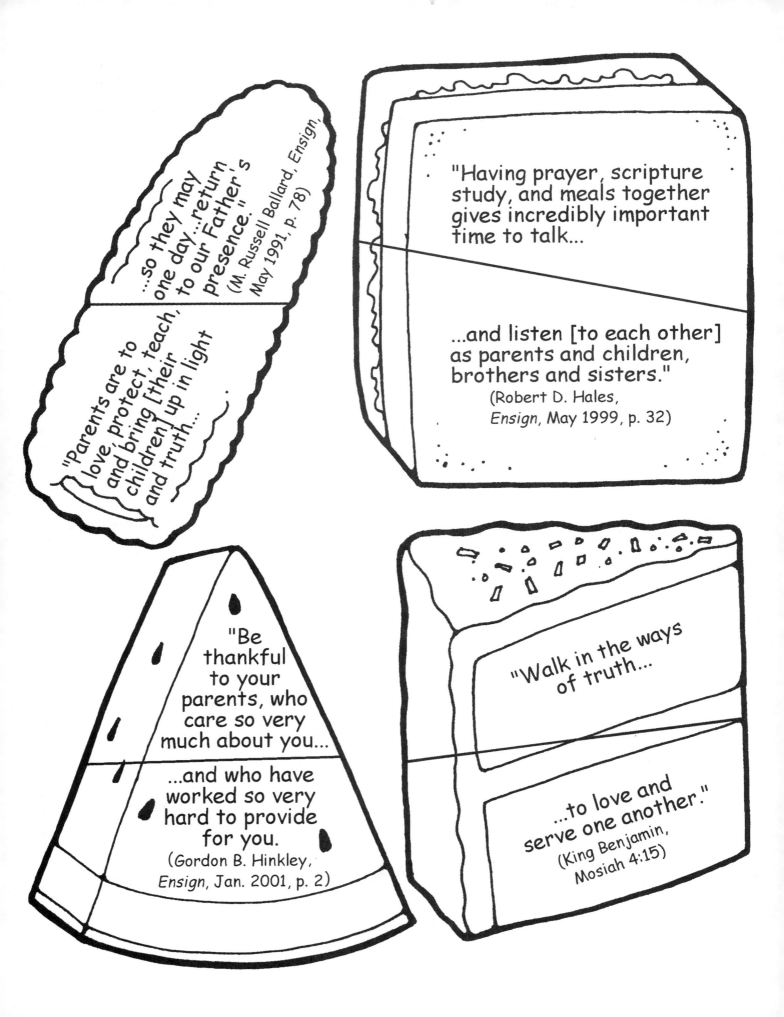

"...so they may one day...return to our Father's presence." (M. Russell Ballard, Ensign, May 1991, p. 78)

"Parents are to love, protect, teach, and bring [their children] up in light and truth...

"Having prayer, scripture study, and meals together gives incredibly important time to talk...

...and listen [to each other] as parents and children, brothers and sisters."
(Robert D. Hales, Ensign, May 1999, p. 32)

"Be thankful to your parents, who care so very much about you...

...and who have worked so very hard to provide for you.
(Gordon B. Hinkley, Ensign, Jan. 2001, p. 2)

"Walk in the ways of truth...

...to love and serve one another."
(King Benjamin, Mosiah 4:15)

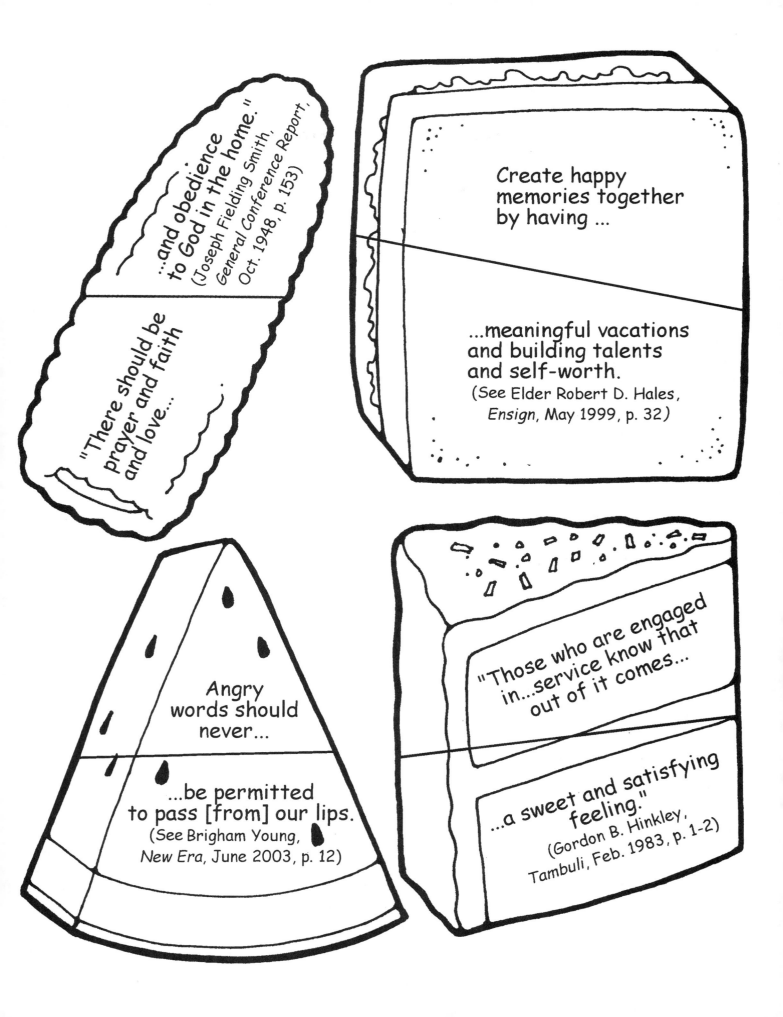

"...and obedience to God in the home." (Joseph Fielding Smith, *General Conference Report*, Oct. 1948, p. 153)

"There should be prayer and faith and love..."

Create happy memories together by having ...

...meaningful vacations and building talents and self-worth. (See Elder Robert D. Hales, *Ensign*, May 1999, p. 32)

Angry words should never...

...be permitted to pass [from] our lips. (See Brigham Young, *New Era*, June 2003, p. 12)

"Those who are engaged in...service know that out of it comes...

...a sweet and satisfying feeling." (Gordon B. Hinkley, *Tambuli*, Feb. 1983, p. 1-2)

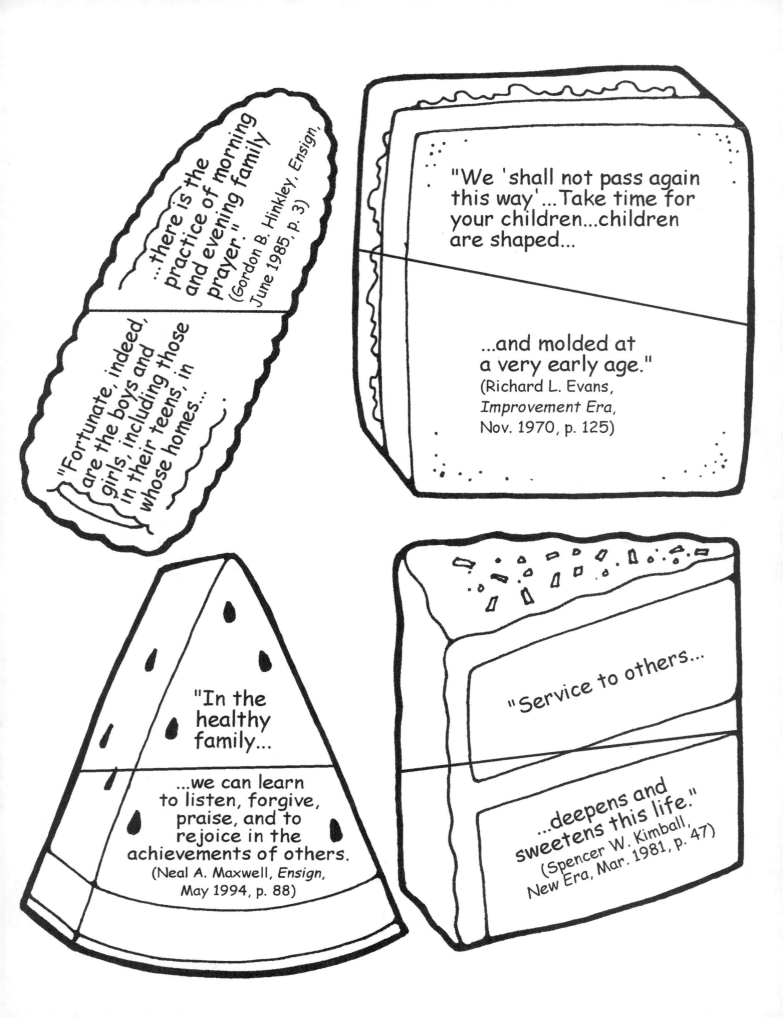

"...there is the practice of morning and evening family prayer." (Gordon B. Hinkley, Ensign, June 1985, p. 3)

"Fortunate, indeed, are the boys and girls, including those in their teens, in whose homes..."

"We 'shall not pass again this way'...Take time for your children...children are shaped...

...and molded at a very early age." (Richard L. Evans, *Improvement Era*, Nov. 1970, p. 125)

"In the healthy family...

...we can learn to listen, forgive, praise, and to rejoice in the achievements of others. (Neal A. Maxwell, *Ensign*, May 1994, p. 88)

"Service to others...

...deepens and sweetens this life." (Spencer W. Kimball, New Era, Mar. 1981, p. 47)

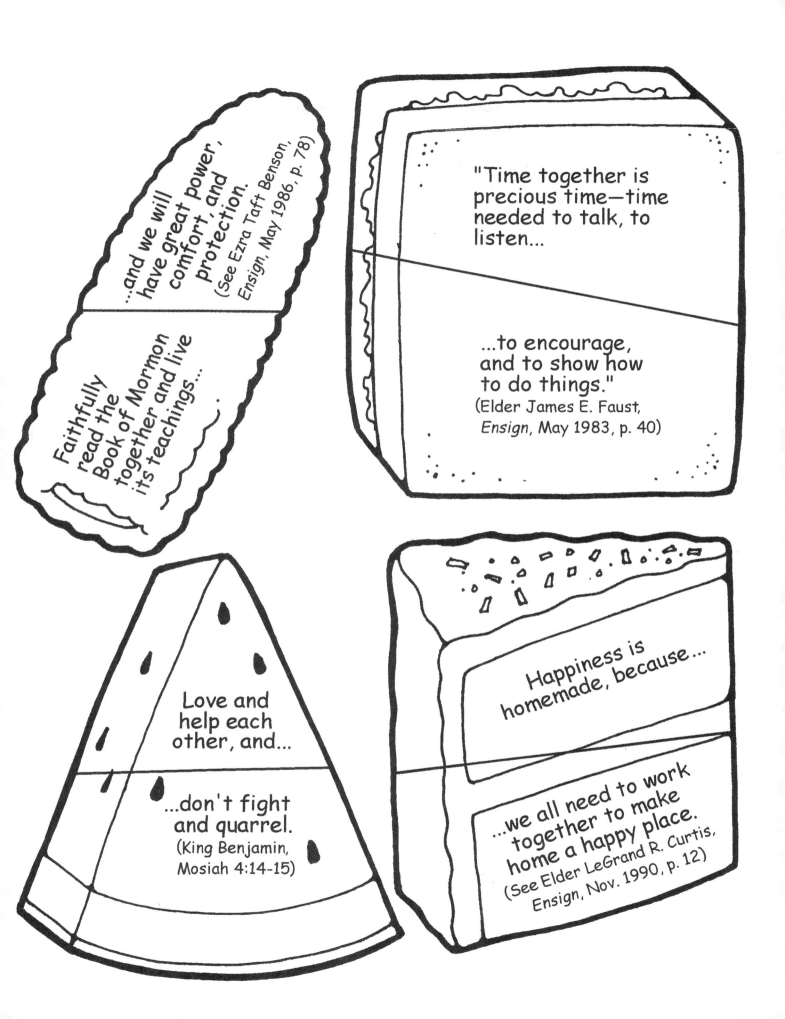

...and we will have great power, comfort, and protection.
(See Ezra Taft Benson, *Ensign*, May 1986, p. 78)

Faithfully read the Book of Mormon together and live its teachings...

"Time together is precious time—time needed to talk, to listen...

...to encourage, and to show how to do things."
(Elder James E. Faust, *Ensign*, May 1983, p. 40)

Love and help each other, and...

...don't fight and quarrel.
(King Benjamin, Mosiah 4:14-15)

Happiness is homemade, because...

...we all need to work together to make home a happy place.
(See Elder LeGrand R. Curtis, *Ensign*, Nov. 1990, p. 12)

Theme 11   Keeping the Sabbath Day Holy Can Strengthen My Family

BiTe-Size MeMoRize

Remember the sabbath day 2 🔑+P it holy.

Exodus 20:8

SCRIPTURE TO MEMORIZE: Memorize the Exodus 20:8 Bite-size Memorize poster on p. 110 (shown right). Give children a copy of the small Bite-size Memorize on page 111 or print from CD-ROM.*

LESSON: Ask, "How does keeping the Sabbath day holy strengthen your family?" Answer this question using the scriptures, Primary lessons, and sources below to teach.

- The Sabbath day is a day to rest from our labors and to worship at church (D&C 59:9; "My Gospel Standards," paragraph 6; *Primary 1—Nursery*, lessons 15, 44; *Primary 3—CTR B*, lesson 40).
- The Sabbath is a day to rest from our labors and to strengthen our family relationships (D&C 59:10; *Primary 2—CTR A*, lesson 37)
- Sharing my testimony brings me closer to Heavenly Father and Jesus (Mosiah 18:9; John 17:3; *Primary 5—D&C*, lesson 46; First Presidency letter, 2 May, 2002)
- Fasting can bring me closer to Heavenly Father and Jesus (Helaman 3:35; D&C 59:14; *Primary 3—CTR B*, lesson 41) *Note:* Young children should not be expected to fast: "Neither should parents compel their little children to fast" (Joseph F. Smith, *Gospel Doctrine,* 244).

MORE IDEAS: See More Sharing-Time Activities (Theme 11) previewed in the back of this book, available in the *Primary Partners® Sharing Time Treasures—My Family Can Be Forever* book or CD-ROM (to print images in color or black and white).

Activity:
My Family Can Keep the Sabbath (Sabbath-Day Scavenger Hunt)

OBJECTIVE: Tell children, "Our family can be strong as we keep the Sabbath Day holy. Let's have a Sabbath-Day Scavenger Hunt to learn ways we can keep the Sabbath Day holy."

TO MAKE VISUALS: *Copy, color, and cut out visuals and *Scavenger-Hunt Clues* (p. 112-117).

TO PRESENT:

1. Tape visuals on the far left of the board or on a wall, or tape visuals under chairs ahead of time. Provide a space on the board to post visuals.

2. From the *Scavenger-Hunt Clues* page, call out two items at a time and have two children find them, saying, for example, "I need the temple, journal, and a pair of shoes" (shown right). Then have them tell how each item can help them keep the Sabbath Day holy. Ideas are found on the *Scavenger-Hunt Clues* page.

*All images can be printed in full color and black and white using the CD-ROM:
Primary Partners Sharing Time—My Family Can Be Forever.

Remember the sabbath day 2 🔑 +p it holy.

Exodus 20:8

Remember the sabbath day 2 🔑+p it holy.

Exodus 20:8

Remember the sabbath day 2 🔑+p it holy.

Exodus 20:8

Remember the sabbath day 2 🔑+p it holy.

Exodus 20:8

Remember the sabbath day 2 🔑+p it holy.

Exodus 20:8

Journal

Family Group Sheet

Family Pedigree

September

Dear Elder Guymon,
I wanted to write and
tell you ... testimony
Africa

Sister Hafen
2061 Harrison
Delta, UT

Love

Elder Garry Guymon
Ivory Coast – West Africa
Church of Jesus Christ
of Latter-day Saints

SCAVENGER-HUNT CLUES:

Call out two items at a time and have two children find them.
Then have them tell how each item can help them keep the Sabbath Day holy.

JOURNAL: Write in your journal.

MISSIONARY LETTER: Write letters or make voice tapes to send to missionaries.

FAMILY PEDIGREE CHART: Write your family history and trace your ancestors.

PAIR OF SHOES: Take a walk together and appreciate Heavenly Father's creations.

JESUS: Partake of the sacrament to remember Jesus. Learn about Jesus and how we can follow His example.

GRANDPARENTS: Visit, call, or write grandparents or visit the elderly.

FAMILY: Spend time with your family. Have family prayer, family council, family home evening, or special dinners together.

MUSIC NOTES: Sing hymns or Primary songs. Listen to Sunday music. Go to or have a family choir practice.

DISHES: Do the dishes together so you can talk and visit.

TITHING ENVELOPE: Pay your tithing so your family will be blessed and you can help build temples and churches.

SCRAPBOOK PAGE: Make scrapbook pages with family photos and other memories.

FOOD: Fast on fast Sunday or have a special fast for a special need.

NUMBER 13: Memorize and recite the 13 articles of faith.

GAME BOARD: Play quiet games with the family.

SICK PERSON: Visit the sick or lonely.

GREETING CARD: Make and send a get-well or greeting card.

TEMPLE: Visit the temple grounds and visitors' center where you can learn more about the gospel and enjoy the beauty.

SCRIPTURES: Read the scriptures together, have devotionals, have a scripture chase, or study and underline important scriptures.

BOOK OF MORMON: Read Book of Mormon stories, or write your testimony and place it in a Book of Mormon with your family photo.

ICE-CREAM CONE: Make homemade ice cream or other treats together.

Theme 12   My Family Is Blessed When We Remember Jesus Christ

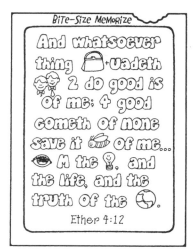

BITE-SIZE MEMORIZE

And whatsoever thing 👜+uadeth 👫 2 do good is of me; 4 good cometh of none save it 🖐 of me... 👁 M the 💡, and the life, and the truth of the 🌍.

Ether 4:12

SCRIPTURE TO MEMORIZE: Memorize the Ether 4:12 Bite-size Memorize poster on p. 119 (shown right). Give children a copy of the small Bite-size Memorize on page 120 or print from CD-ROM.*

LESSON: Ask, "How are our families blessed when we remember Jesus?" Answer this question using the scriptures, Primary lessons, and sources below to teach.

- I remember Jesus when I partake of the sacrament (3 Nephi 18:7, 11; Matthew 26:26-28; *Primary 1—Nursery*, lesson 40; *Primary 3—CTR B*, lessons 32-33).
- Heavenly Father planned for Jesus to be born into a family (Luke 2:1-20; Matthew 2:1-13; *Primary 1—Nursery*, lesson 46; *Primary 3—CTR B*, lesson 47).
- What Gifts can I give to Jesus (John 14:15; Matthew 25:40; Mosiah 2:17; *Primary 3— CTR B*, lesson 37)?
- Jesus Christ will come again (Matthew 16:27; *Primary 2—CTR A*, lesson 43).

MORE IDEAS: See More Sharing-Time Activities (Theme 12) previewed in the back of this book, available in the *Primary Partners® Sharing Time Treasures—My Family Can Be Forever* book or CD-ROM (to print images in color or black and white).

Activity: Trimming the Family Christmas Tree (Gifts-to-Jesus Seek-a-Service Match Game)

OBJECTIVE: Tell children, "Our families are blessed when we remember Jesus. Let's find gifts of service placed under the tree that we can give to our family. When we give the gifts of service to our family it is like giving gifts to Jesus."

TO MAKE VISUALS: *Copy, color, and cut out visuals (p. 121-127), mounting tree on a poster and laminating the entire poster. Laminate and cut out gifts and ornaments, cutting ornaments in half. Using double-stick tape, mount one half of each ornament on the back side of the gifts. Put the matching halves of the ornaments in a container to draw from, or tape them to the wall or board for children to choose from. Tape the folded tab, on the bottom of the gifts, to the board. Tape the top of each gift with double-stick tape (so gifts can be flipped down to view ornaments behind gifts).

TO PRESENT: (1) Divide children into teams or play individually, taking turns drawing an ornament piece and flipping the gifts down to find the matching piece.
(2) To make a match, have players take turns turning one gift over to find the match to the ornament. If they don't find it on the first gift, the other team can choose a gift. If not, it reverts back to the first team to guess. (3) When a match is made, read the service gift and place the ornament on the tree. (4) Award a point to each team who finds a match, then total the points to determine the winning team.

*All images can be printed in full color and black and white using the CD-ROM:
Primary Partners Sharing Time—My Family Can Be Forever.

118

And whatsoever thing 👜 +uadeth 2 do good is of me; 4 good cometh of none save it 🐝 of me... 👁 M the 💡, and the life, and the truth of the 🌎.

Ether 4:12

And whatsoever thing 🛍 +Uadeth 👧👦 2 do good is Of me; 4 good cometh of none save it 🐝 of me... 👁 M the 💡, and the life, and the truth of the 🌍.

Ether 4:12

And whatsoever thing 🛍 +Uadeth 👧👦 2 do good is Of me; 4 good cometh of none save it 🐝 of me... 👁 M the 💡, and the life, and the truth of the 🌍.

Ether 4:12

And whatsoever thing 🛍 +Uadeth 👧👦 2 do good is Of me; 4 good cometh of none save it 🐝 of me... 👁 M the 💡, and the life, and the truth of the 🌍.

Ether 4:12

And whatsoever thing 🛍 +Uadeth 👧👦 2 do good is Of me; 4 good cometh of none save it 🐝 of me... 👁 M the 💡, and the life, and the truth of the 🌍.

Ether 4:12

Cut carefully along the inside of the dotted line.

Cut carefully along the inside of the dotted line.

Do not cut along the dotted line. Use this margin to mount the other side.

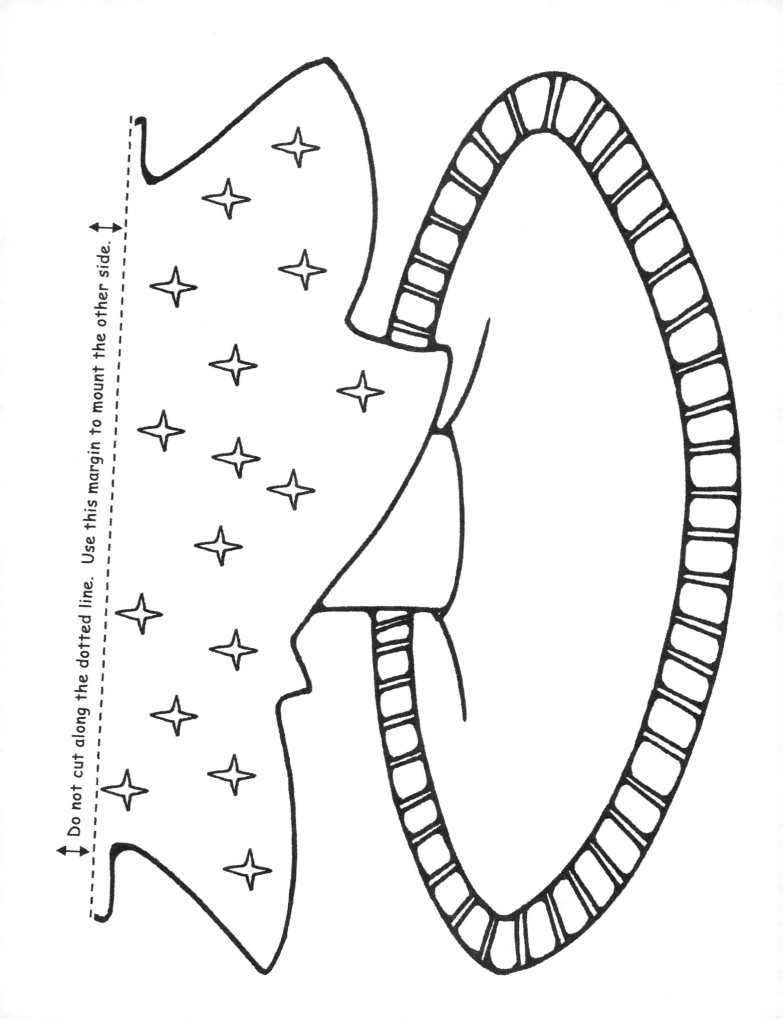

Do not cut along the dotted line. Use this margin to mount the other side.

GIFTS

Fold under and tape to board.

TO

Fold under and tape to board.

I helped my mom without delay...

...and quickly put the dishes away.

I made a special thank you card...

...to give to my father who works so hard.

...for teaching me a Primary song.

I gave a big hug to my mom...

JESUS

Fold under and tape to board.

MORE SHARING-TIME ACTIVITIES:
Primary Partners ® Sharing Time Treasures

The following *Sharing Time Treasures* suggest more ideas for Sharing-Time Themes 1-12 for the 2004 theme: "My Family Can Be Forever."

We have made it easier for you to access all of the following 87 activities (previewed as follows) without purchasing the following eight *Primary Partners* activity books and CD-ROMs that coordinate with the *Primary 1-7 Manuals*):
Primary Partners Nursery and Age 3, Volumes 1 and 2;
Primary Partners CTR-A and *Primary Partners CTR-B;*
Primary Partners Ages 8-12: New Testament, Old Testament,
Book of Mormon, and *Doctrine and Covenants*

We have combined all of the activities shown on the following pages in one book and CD-ROM (with full-color or black-and-white images).

To use the following previewed activities, simply do one of two things.
Choice 1: Copy the activities found in the <u>one</u> *Primary Partners Sharing Time Treasures* book (shown right) or print them from the *Primary Partners Sharing Time Treasures* CD-ROM.
Choice 2: Copy these select activities from the <u>eight</u> *Primary Partners* books (listed above), or print from the CD-ROMs available for each book.

• For large sharing-time groups, enlarge the activities for group presentations.

Theme 1: I Am a Child of God #1-8

1. Heavenly Family Photo in *Primary Partners CTR-A,* lesson 3

2. Heavenly Father's Plan—I Am a Child of God (Face Fun) in *Primary Partners Nursery,* Vol. 2, lesson 3

3. Connect the Dots of Jesus Praying—*Primary Partners CTR-B,* lesson 19

Copy the above images from the *Primary Partners Sharing Time Treasures—My Family Can Be Forever* book, or print in color or black and white from the CD-ROM. Or, copy or print the images from the corresponding *Primary Partners* books or CD-ROMs.

Theme 1: I Am a Child of God #1-8
Theme 2: the Family Is Central to Heavenly Father's Plan #9-13

4. Temple Eternity Wheel in *Primary Partners CTR-B*, lesson 35

5. Paper Dolls with Heavenly and Earthly Home in *Primary Partners Nursery*, Vol. 1, lesson 3

6. Heavenly Father and Jesus Love Me Hearts On-a-String in *Primary Partners Nursery*, Vol. 2, lesson 6

7. Heavenly Father Loves Me Picture and Mirror in *Primary Partners Nursery*, Vol. 1, lesson 6

8. Child of God Paper Dolls in *Primary Partners Nursery,* Vol. 1, lesson 1

9. Families Are Special Missing Family Puzzle in *Primary Partners CTR-A*, lesson 6

10. Families Temple Prep Slide Show in *Primary Partners Nursery*, Vol. 2, lesson 26

11. Parents Help Me Learn Commandments Slide Show in *Primary Partners CTR-B*, lesson 28

12. I Can "Bee" Obedient Meter in Primary Partners CTR-B, lesson 39

13. Priesthood Blessings Spiral Kite in *Primary Partners CTR-B*, lesson 9

14. Premortal Life Puppet Show in *Primary Partners CTR-A*, lesson 4

15. Heavenly Father's Plan of Salvation Storyboard and Quiz in *Primary Partners Old Testament*, lesson 1

Copy the above images from the *Primary Partners Sharing Time Treasures—My Family Can Be Forever* book, or print in color or black and white from the CD-ROM. Or, copy or print the images from the corresponding *Primary Partners* books or CD-ROMs.

Theme 3: Jesus Makes it Possible for Me to Live with Heavenly Father Again #14-21
Theme 4: Families Can Be Happy When They Follow Jesus #22-27

16. My Faith Grows Premortal Life, Earth Life Quiz in *Primary Partners D&C*, lesson 28

17. Repentance Wheel in *Primary Partners CTR-B*, lesson 22

18. Atonement Object Lesson in *Primary Partners Old Testament*, lesson 45

19. What Would Jesus Do? Choice Situation Sack in *Primary Partners Book of Mormon*, lesson 8

20. Peer Pressure Cross Match Puzzle in *Primary Partners Old Testament*, lesson 32

21. Decision Drama in *Primary Partners Old Testament*, lesson 16

22. Holy Ghost Gift Box in *Primary Partners CTR-B*, lesson 12

23. Book of Mormon Promise in *Primary Partners Book of Mormon*, lesson 44

24. I Choose to Follow Jesus Reward List in *Primary Partners Old Testament*, lesson 23

25. Heavenly Treasure Hunt in *Primary Partners CTR-A*, lesson 30

26. My Gospel Standards Sentence Search in *Primary Partners Old Testament*, lesson 47

27. Strong Spirit Poster in *Primary Partners New Testament*, lesson 7

Copy the above images from the *Primary Partners Sharing Time Treasures—My Family Can Be Forever* book, or print in color or black and white from the CD-ROM. Or, copy or print the images from the corresponding *Primary Partners* books or CD-ROMs.

Theme 5: Family Members Have Important Responsibilities #28-33
Theme 6: Heavenly Father Teaches Me How to Strengthen My Family #34-41

28. Birds of a Feather Stick Together Family Fun in *Primary Partners Nursery*, Vol. 1, lesson 23

29. Young Joseph Puzzle in *Primary Partners CTR-B*, lesson 4

30. Stripling Warriors—Parents Thank-You Card in *Primary Partners Book of Mormon*, lesson 27

31. "Bee" Obedient Meter in *Primary Partners CTR-B*, lesson 39

32. Family Example Ice-Cream Sundae in Primary Partners CTR-B, less. 45

33. Family Face Block Game in *Primary Partners Nursery*, Vol. 1, lesson 23

34. Gratitude Gopher's Grab Bag Game in *Primary Partners CTR-A*, lesson 24

35. Family Prayer Fan in *Primary Partners Nursery*, Vol. 1, lesson 27

36. Scripture Blessings Sticker Challenge in *Primary Partners Old Testament*, lesson 37

37. Strengthen My Family—Sheep and Goat Situation Slap Game in Primary Partners New Testament, lesson 27

38. Shipshape Family Goal Chart in Primary Partners Book of Mormon, lesson 6

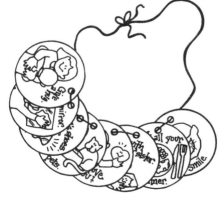

39. Kind Deeds Advent Necklace in *Primary Partners Nursery*, Vol. 2, lesson 46

Copy the above images from the *Primary Partners Sharing Time Treasures—My Family Can Be Forever* book, or print in color or black and white from the CD-ROM. Or, copy or print the images from the corresponding *Primary Partners* books or CD-ROMs.

40. Service Station Sack of Reminders in *Primary Partners D&C*, lesson 39

41. Spiritual Strength—Sink or Swim Slide Show in *Primary Partners Old Testament*, less. 25

42. I Promise and Heavenly Father Promises—Two-Sided Puzzle in *Primary Partners CTR-B*, lesson 13

43. Child's Photo in Temple Frame in *Primary Partners D&C*, lesson 35

44. Mission Statements Match Game in *Primary Partners Old Testament*, lesson 18

45. Families Forever Temple Tie and Tithing Purse in *Primary Partners Nursery*, Vol. 1, lesson 26

46. Temple Eternity Wheel in *Primary Partners CTR-B*, less. 35

47. Family Tree Picture Stickers in *Primary Partners Nursery*, Vol. 1, lesson 25

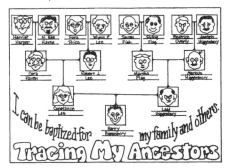

48. Tracing Ancestors Pedigree Chart in *Primary Partners D&C*, lesson 34

49. Miracles of Jesus Picture Poster in *Primary Partners New Testament*, less. 16.

50. "Jesus Is My Light" Light Switch Cover in *Primary Partners CTR-B*, lesson 7

51. Connect the Dots of Jesus Praying—*Primary Partners CTR-B*, lesson 19

Copy the above images from the *Primary Partners Sharing Time Treasures—My Family Can Be Forever* book, or print in color or black and white from the CD-ROM. Or, copy or print the images from the corresponding *Primary Partners* books or CD-ROMs.

Theme 8: Faith, Prayer, Repentance, and Forgiveness Can Strengthen My Family #49-56

Theme 9: Respect, Love, Work, and Wholesome Recreation Can Strengthen My Family #57-65

52. Shipshape Family Goal Chart in *Primary Partners Book of Mormon*, lesson 6

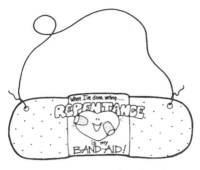

53. Repentance Heals—Bandage Breastplate in *Primary Partners CTR-B*, lesson 10

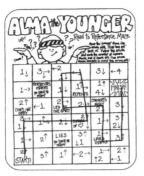

54. Alma the Younger's Road to Repentance Maze in *Primary Partners Book of Mormon*, lesson 14

55. Forgiving Faces in *Primary Partners CTR-A*, lesson 40

56. Merciful and Forgiving Scripture Search in *Primary Partners New Testament*, less. 22

57. Respectful Choices Poster in *Primary Partners New Testament*, lesson 8

58. Love and Compassion Wheel in *Primary Partners New Testament*, lesson 13

59. My Circle of Love Spin-and-Serve Game in *Primary Partners Old Testament*, lesson 10

60. Good Samaritan Show-and-Tell in *Primary Partners Nursery*, Vol. 2, less. 34

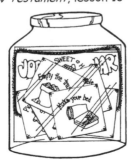

61. Job Jar with Jobs in *Primary Partners Nursery*, Vol. 1, less. 31

62. Pocketful of Humble Deeds Secret Service in *Primary Partners Book of Mormon*, lesson 21

63. Share Time, Talent, Means—Consecration Checkbook in *Primary Partners D&C*, lesson 18

Copy the above images from the *Primary Partners Sharing Time Treasures—My Family Can Be Forever* book, or print in color or black and white from the CD-ROM. Or, copy or print the images from the corresponding *Primary Partners* books or CD-ROMs.

Theme 9:　Respect, Love, Work, and Wholesome Recreation Can Strengthen My Family #57-65
Theme 10:　Prophets Teach Me How to Strengthen My Family #66-72
Theme 11: Keeping the Sabbath Day Can Strengthen My Family #73-80

64. My Ant Farm Leisure-Time Log in *Young Women Fun-tastic! Manual 2*, lesson 43

65. Prophet Poster in *Primary Partners Nursery*, Vol. 1 lesson 43

66. Prophets Teach Us—Make a Prophet Poster *Primary Partners CTR-B*, lesson 8

67. Commandments Key Word Cake in *Primary Partners Old Testament*, lesson 21

68. Armor of God—Fight for Right Word Choice in *Primary Partners Book of Mormon*, lesson 25

69. Moroni and Me Personal Golden Plates in *Primary Partners Book of Mormon*, lesson 42

70. My Personal Title of Liberty in *Primary Partners Book of Mormon*, lesson 25

71. Blessings Blockbuster Game in *Primary Partners Old Testament*, lesson 35

72. The Prophet Guides Choices & Consequences Cross Match in *Primary Partners D&C*, lesson 31

73. Sunday Block Game in *Primary Partners CTR-B*, lesson 40

74. Sabbath Day Advent Calendar in *Primary Partners Old Testament*, lesson 20

75. Sabbath Day Decision Drama or Draw in *Primary Partners D&C*, lesson 41

Copy the above images from the *Primary Partners Sharing Time Treasures—My Family Can Be Forever* book, or print in color or black and white from the CD-ROM. Or, copy or print the images from the corresponding *Primary Partners* books or CD-ROMs.

Theme 11: Keeping the Sabbath Day Can Strengthen My Family #73-80
Theme 12: My Family Is Blessed When We Remember Jesus Christ #81-87

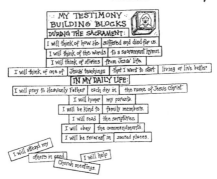

76. Testimony Building Blocks in *Primary Partners New Test.*, lesson 29

77. Bear Testimony Secret Message Poster in *Primary Partners New Testament*, lesson 37

78. "Bear" Testimony—Slide Show/Doorknob Hanger in *Primary Partners D&C*, lesson 9

79. Fasting Tree in *Primary Partners CTR-B*, lesson 41

80. Fasting and Prayer Bring Blessings—Blessings Puzzle in *Primary Partners Old Test.*, lesson 38

81. Remember Jesus—Sacrament Manners Match Game in *Primary Partners Nursery*, Vol. 1, lesson 40

82. Testimony Building Blocks Puzzle in *Primary Partners New Testament*, lesson 29 (same as #76 above)

83. Moveable Manger Scene in *Primary Partners, Nursery*, Vol. 1, lesson 46

84. Love for Jesus—Word Picture Story in *Primary Partners CTR-B*, lesson 36

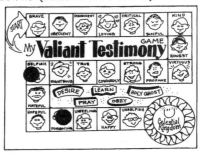

85. Valiant Testimony Board Game in *Primary Partners Old Testament*, lesson 41

86. Millennium Match Game in *Primary Partners Old Testament*, lesson 36

87. Second Coming Checklist in *Primary Partners New Testament*, lesson 46

Copy the above images from the *Primary Partners Sharing Time Treasures—My Family Can Be Forever* book, or print in color or black and white from the CD-ROM. Or, copy or print the images from the corresponding *Primary Partners* books or CD-ROMs.

Preview of More Sharing-time Activities
for the 2004 Sharing-time
Theme: My Family Can Be Forever

In Full Color and Ready to Use!
From *Gospel Fun Activities* book and CD-ROM

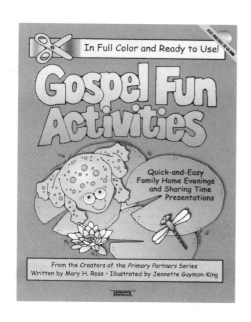

Gospel Fun Activities #3 Commandments: I Can Return to My Heavenly Father (Commandment Maze). Use for sharing-time themes 9 and 10.

Gospel Fun Activities #4 Faith: My Faith Can Grow (Choices: Strong-and-Wilting-Plant Match Game). Use for sharing-time theme 8.

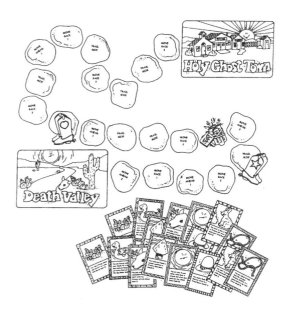

Gospel Fun Activities #6 Holy Ghost: The Holy Ghost Will Help Me Choose the Right (Trail-to-Holy-Ghost-Town Game). Use for sharing-time theme 4.

Gospel Fun Activities #5 Follow Jesus: I Will Always Remember Jesus (Find-the-Light Situation Spotlight). Use for sharing-time theme 4.

Preview of More Sharing-time Activities

Gospel Fun Activities #9 Repentance: Repentance Can Make Us Happy (Happy Henry and Miserable Mack Body-Building Puzzles). Use for sharing-time themes 3, and 8.

Gospel Fun Activities #12 Testimony: I Will Build My House Upon the Rock of Jesus Christ (Testimony Rocks to Build a Sure Foundation). Use for sharing-time themes 11 and 12.

Gospel Fun Activities #11 Service: I Will Love and Serve Others (My-Service-Garden Game to Plant Acts of Service). Use for sharing-time theme 6 and 9.

Gospel Fun Activities #10 Second-Coming: I Will Be Ready to Meet Jesus When He Comes Again (Second-Coming Suitcase). Use for sharing-time theme 12.

2004 Singing Fun Motivators:

In minutes you can help children learn the songs for the 2004 sharing-time theme: "My Family Can Be Forever." With this *Primary Partners Singing Fun* book you can teach the eight or more practice songs using visuals and starter words for each verse. Plus you will find activities to motivate children to sing. These are also available on CD-ROM to print images in color or black and white.

New "Faith in God" Activity Days Program:

With this book of ready-to-apply goal activities, you can help girls ages 8-11 achieve over 30 goals designed for them in the new "Faith in God" Activity Days Program. *Primary Partners "Faith in God" We Love Activity Days* book has over 30 detailed activity plans. Girls can reach their "Learning and Living the Gospel," "Serving Others," and "Developing Talents" goals. All activities can be copied from the book or printed from the CD-ROM in full color or black and white.

Enjoy Full-color, Ready-to-use Singing Fun Motivators:

With these colored, ready-to-use visuals you can motivate children to sing in a fun way. Use them for family home evening, classroom fun, and Primary singing time. They are also available on CD-ROM to print images in color or black and white.

BOOK 1: SUPER SINGING ACTIVITIES

In *Super Singing Activities* you'll find: Melody's Family Tree, Bird in the Leafy Treetops, Build a Snowman, Christmas Sing with Me, City of Enoch Singing Meter, Fill Noah's Ark Pick-a-song, and more.

BOOK 2: SUPER LITTLE SINGERS

In *Super Little Singers* you'll find singing motivators, visuals, and action activities for 28 songs (21 from the *Children's Songbook*). You'll love the visuals for seven all-time favorite children's songs, e.g., "Ants Go Marching," "Eensy Weensy Spider," "Five Little Ducks," "Five Little Speckled Frogs," "Old MacDonald," "Twinkle, Twinkle, Little Star," and "Wheels on the Bus."